Postmodernizing
the Faith

Other Titles by Millard Erickson

Postmodernizing
the Faith

Evangelical Responses
to the Challenge of Postmodernism

Millard J. Erickson

Baker Books
A Division of Baker Book House Co
Grand Rapids, Michigan 49516

Published by Baker Books
a Division of Baker Book House Company
P.O. Box 6287, Grand Rapids, MI 49516-6287

Printed in the United States of America

Library of Congress Cataloging-in-Publication Data

Erickson, Millard J.
 Postmodernizing the faith : evangelical responses to the challenge of
postmodernism / Millard J. Erickson.
  p. cm.
 Includes bibliographical references and index.
 ISBN 0-8010-2164-2 (pbk.)
  1. Theology, Doctrinal—History—20th century. 2. Postmodernism—
Religious aspects—Christianity. 3. Evangelicalism. I. Title.
 BT28.E73 1998
 261.5′1—dc21   97-38493

For more information about academic books, resources for Christian leaders, and all
new releases available from Baker Book House, visit our web site:
http://www.bakerbooks.com

To E. Earle Ellis
Research Professor of Theology, Southwestern Baptist Seminary
A friend with whom every conversation has been a learning experience.

Contents

Preface

When I first began writing about postmodernism in 1990, there was relatively little being produced on that topic by evangelicals. All of that has changed, however. Large numbers of evangelical thinkers are aware of this development, which some believe should be considered a paradigm shift, and are formulating responses to it.

The purpose of this little volume is to survey some representative evangelical responses to postmodernism. These range from those who very strongly reject it to those who embrace it almost completely. Although each understands postmodernism somewhat differently, it is apparent that they are discussing the same phenomenon. The nature of the evangelicalism that each espouses also varies somewhat from one to another. It is our hope that the study of the efforts of these several representatives will help introduce the reader to postmodernism and will also stimulate thinking and response. This is also the first step in a much more thorough analysis and response to postmodernism which I am developing.

Portions of this manuscript have been presented in lecture form. Chapters 2, 3, 4, and 5 formed the content of the Sizemore Lectures at Midwestern Baptist Theological Seminary, Kansas City, Missouri, November 5–8, 1996, and the Staley Lectures at Southwest Baptist University, Bolivar, Missouri, February 24–26, 1997. Chapter 1 was presented in somewhat different form as the academic lecture at the inauguration of David S. Dockery as president of Union University, Jackson, Tennessee, October 16, 1996, and chapter 8 is adapted from a presentation in a panel at the annual meeting of the Evangelical Philosophical Society in Philadelphia, November 16, 1995. The feedback received on those occasions has been of great help to me in refining some of the thoughts contained therein. Maria denBoer has improved the copy by her skillful editorial work.

Part 1

Introduction

1
The Challenge of Postmodernism

Although the present day is characterized by a great diversity of opinion, there is widespread agreement that our world is changing—and changing rapidly. Whether one considers this phenomenon of change a good or a bad thing, it is virtually impossible to deny its reality. Further, this change is taking place at an accelerating pace. The present intellectual atmosphere has come to be known as postmodernism. Although there are rather widely differing understandings of what postmodernism is, there is significant agreement that it is real and that it is increasingly impinging on our lives.

In one sense, postmodernity is simply that which follows the modern period. That characterization would identify it much like Aristotle's *Metaphysics*, as that which came after the *Physics*. But if we accept this chronological criterion, we encounter a strange problem. For by definition, modern is what is now, or new, and there really could not be a postmodern, only something different that is modern. It appears that even the temporal identification of postmodernism is a mixed matter, that it is that ideology which follows temporally on the ideology of the period that has been designated "modern," in contrast with the "premodern." Some of my readers are probably already rolling their eyes, wondering when this abstruse discussion will end. Yet, postmodernism may be more familiar to us than we realize, something we experience but without the label. We may be like the elderly church member who rose to speak at a church business meeting. The board was proposing the purchase of a new chandelier, and this gentleman expressed his opposition for three reasons. "We can't afford it," he said. "No one can spell it. And furthermore, what we really need is a new light fixture."

A shift in focus may help bring the discussion into sharper view. Let me do so by the use of a couple of thought experiments. The first is a parable, in the form of a question in a music test, as it might be asked at different points in history. It was given to me by a music teacher a few years ago.

1930 Define rhythm
1960 The movement of music in time, including tempo and meter, is called _____.
1990 The movement of music in time, including tempo and meter, is called:
      a. melody
      b. harmony
      c. rhythm
      d. interval
2000 The movement of music in time, commonly called Rhythm, makes you feel:
      a. I don't understand the question
      b. I think this is an unfair question
      c. I don't know what the word Rhythm means
      d. It doesn't matter how I feel, as long as it is my own authentic feeling

If you selected the year 2000 question and chose answer (d), you may be a postmodernist!

The second thought experiment derives from a recent personal experience. I saw a young administrator at the school where I taught at that time entering the building where his office was. He was carrying his lunch and was dressed for the day's work. He was wearing an attractive sport coat, dress shirt, and necktie—and faded blue jeans and athletic shoes! My first reaction was, "The bottom half of him does not fit with the top half!" I realized, however, that I had just had a modern reaction, based on the idea that there should be consistency in one's dress, as well as in one's thoughts.

Historical Background

These two considerations may help us begin to gain a feel for the general cultural pervasiveness of postmodernism. In general, postmodernism is understood as an intellectual movement growing out of and supplanting modernism. It can be best understood in terms of its contrast with the periods that preceded it.

Premodernism

If the modern period was the period following the Enlightenment, then what preceded it was the premodern, including the medieval and ancient periods. As varied as were the ideas during this long premodern period of time, there are certain common elements. One was a belief in the rationality of the universe. There also was a belief that observable nature was not the whole of reality. There was usually something of a dualism, involving an unseen component of reality. In religious views, this was a supernaturalism, a belief in the existence of a god or gods. In less overtly religious views, this took a different form of expression. For Plato, for example, reality was most fundamentally found in the Forms or Ideas, the pure essences of which concrete entities were shadows or reflections.

The premodern understanding of reality was teleological. There was believed to be a purpose or purposes in the universe, within which humans fit and were to be understood. This purpose was being worked out within the world. In the Western tradition, this was the belief that an omnipotent, omniscient God had created the entire universe and the human race, and had a plan he was bringing about. There had to be reasons for things, and these were not limited to efficient or "because of" causes, but also included final or "in order that" causes. This understanding carried over to the interpretation of history. There was a pattern to history, which was outside it. The aim of the historian, or at least the philosopher of history, was to detect this pattern and thus be able to predict the future direction of history.

There were definite metaphysical and epistemological conceptions involved in premodernism. There was a basic belief in the objective existence of the physical world. There also was a belief in a correspondence theory of truth: propositions are true if they correctly describe the realities they purport to describe, false if they do not. This is closely wrapped up with a referential understanding of language. Language does not simply refer to other language, but to something extralinguistic.

Modernism

Premodernism and its mentality were supplanted by modernism, which retained and modified some of these features while also diverging from this approach in some major ways. It shared the belief in metaphysical realism, the correspondence view of truth, and the referential theory of language. It also held that there was a discernible pattern to history. It was, however, in the identification of the reasons for these ideas that divergence from the premodern period became apparent. For example, the transcendent conception of reality was abandoned. Rather than being located above or beyond history, its reason and pattern were found within it. The forces that drive history were, in other words, believed to be immanent within it. This was a type of dualism in some cases, but it was a horizontal dualism. Rather than there being a reality above or beyond observable natural objects, there was something within or behind the phenomena, such as in Immanuel Kant's noumenal world, or the things in themselves. Like premoderns, modern persons were looking for all-inclusive explanations of events and of reality, but believed that this could be done without recourse to anything supernatural.

Final causes or purposes were eliminated by modernism. In their place were put efficient causes. Thus, events that happen in the natural world occur not because of the will of some unseen deity, but because of physical or social realities that bring them about.

Several salient features of modernism should be noted.

1. Naturalism. Reality is believed to be restricted to the observable system of nature. Its immanent laws are the cause of all that occurs.
2. Humanism. The human is the highest reality and value, the end for which all of reality exists rather than the means to the service of some higher being.
3. The scientific method. Knowledge is good and can be attained by humans. The method best suited for this enterprise is the scientific method, which came to fruition during this period. Observation and experimentation are the sources from which our knowledge of truth is built up.
4. Reductionism. From being considered the best means for gaining knowledge, the scientific method came increasingly to be considered the only method, so that various disciplines sought to attain the objectivity and precision of the natural sciences. Humans in some cases were regarded as nothing but highly developed animals.

5. Progress. Because knowledge is good, humanly attainable, and growing, we are progressively overcoming the problems that have beset the human race.

6. Nature. Rather than being fixed and static, nature came to be thought of as dynamic, growing, and developing. Thus it was able to produce the changes in life forms through immanent processes of evolution, rather than requiring explanation in terms of a creator and designer.

7. Certainty. Because knowledge was seen as objective, it could attain certainty. This required foundationalism, the belief that it is possible to base knowledge on some sort of absolute first principles. One early model of this was found in the rationalism of René Descartes, who found one indubitable belief, namely, that he was doubting, and then proceeded to draw deductions from that. An alternative was empiricism, the belief that there are purely objective sensory data from which knowledge can be formulated.

8. Determinism. There was a belief that what happened in the universe followed from fixed causes. Thus, the scientific method could discover these laws of regularity that controlled the universe. Not only physical occurrences but human behavior were believed to be under this etiological control.

9. Individualism. The ideal of the knower was the solitary individual, carefully protecting his or her objectivity by weighing all options. Truth being objective, individuals can discover it by their own efforts. They can free themselves from the conditioning particularities of their own time and place and know reality as it is in itself.

10. Anti-authoritarianism. The human was considered the final and most complete measure of truth. Any externally imposed authority, whether that of the group or of a supernatural being, must be subjected to scrutiny and criticism by human reason.

Modernism can actually be clustered into two general types, a more moderate form and a more extreme form, which I term soft modernism and hard modernism, respectively. Soft modernism shares with its forerunner, premodernism, belief in the rationality of the universe and in human ability to know and understand the truth. Both believe that inclusive explanations of reality, or in other words, integrative metaphysical schemes or worldviews, can be constructed. Hard modernism goes beyond its soft counterpart, however, by excluding anything other than this. On the terms of hard modernism, reality is limited to what can be experienced, thus excluding supernaturalism of any kind. Knowledge is restricted to what can be known through reason and experience, excluding any sort of intuition. What is not logical is not considered real.

The Tenets of Postmodernism

This modern period has, in turn, given way to the postmodern, and its ideology to postmodernism. This represents the convergence of several movements in different intellectual disciplines. In many ways, the beginning inspiration was from the French school of literary criticism known as deconstruction. In history, there is the new historicism, in which history is not merely the objective discovery of the past, but actually creates it. In philosophy, neo-pragmatism holds that words refer not to objective, extralinguistic entities, but to other words. Certain basic motifs have emerged, countering the modern view. Although these will be described at greater length by several of the thinkers we will examine, they can be briefly summarized here.

1. The objectivity of knowledge is denied. Whether the knower is conditioned by the particularities of his or her situation or theories are used oppressively, knowledge is not a neutral means of discovery.
2. Knowledge is uncertain. Foundationalism, the idea that knowledge can be erected on some sort of bedrock of indubitable first principles, has had to be abandoned.
3. All-inclusive systems of explanation, whether metaphysical or historical, are impossible, and the attempt to construct them should be abandoned.
4. The inherent goodness of knowledge is also questioned. The belief that by means of discovering the truths of nature it could be controlled and evil and ills overcome has been disproved by the destructive ends to which knowledge has been put (in warfare, for instance).

5. Thus, progress is rejected. The history of the twentieth century should make this clear.
6. The model of the isolated individual knower as the ideal has been replaced by community-based knowledge. Truth is defined by and for the community, and all knowledge occurs within some community.
7. The scientific method as the epitomization of the objective method of inquiry is called into question. Truth is not known simply through reason, but through other channels, such as intuition.

Corresponding to the two types of modernism are, accordingly, two varieties of postmodernism, which, interestingly enough, I would also label as "hard" and "soft." Soft postmodernism rejects those extremes of modernism found in hard modernism: the dogmatic naturalism and antisupernaturalism; the reductionistic view of reason, which reduces psychology to biology, biology to chemistry, and chemistry to physics. It rejects the limitation of knowledge to sense experience, and the meaningful use of language to those statements for which we can identify sense perceptions that would verify or falsify them. It rejects the restriction of the understanding of human personality as a set of stimulus–response reactions. It rejects the type of naive objectivity that denies the effect of historical and cultural situations. In other words, it rejects logical positivism, behaviorism, and all other artificially scientistic approaches to reality.

Hard postmodernism, best represented by deconstruction, goes beyond this to reject the idea of any sort of objectivity and rationality. It maintains that all theories are simply worked out to justify and empower those who hold them, rather than being based on facts. It not only rejects the limitation of meaning of language to empirical reference; it rejects the idea that language has any sort of objective or extralinguistic reference at all. It moves from relativism to pluralism in truth. Not only is all knowing and all speaking done from a particular perspective, but each perspective is equally true or valuable. The meaning of a statement is not to be found objectively in the meaning intended by the speaker or writer, but is the meaning that the hearer or reader finds in it. "What it means to me" is its meaning, even if that is quite different than what it says to you.

19

I would propose, as a Christian and a theologian, that the presence of soft postmodernism is encouraging to Christians. It opens the door for believers to contend for the truth of the Christian faith, in contrast to a secular world that formerly excluded any faith of this type. What may not be so apparent is the threat hard postmodernism poses to the cause of Christianity.

In the following chapters, we examine six evangelical responses to this phenomenon of postmodernism. These vary in the degree to which their assessment of postmodernism is positive. In general, the chapters progress from extreme rejection to extreme acceptance of postmodernism. The first three thinkers basically contend that the contemporary trends known as postmodernism are incompatible with genuine Christian faith and must therefore be rejected. The latter three believe that postmodernism is a development that needs to be accepted, and that Christian theology must be done in light of it and incorporate at least some of its tenets. Then, after learning from different styles of response, we propose the beginning of a response of our own, a suggestion of the directions in which a future response to postmodernism should move.

Part 2

Negative Responses to Postmodernism

2
Just Say "No"!

David Wells

The work of David Wells represents one of the most thoroughgoing analyses of modern culture by an evangelical in our time. It also is unique in its criticism of contemporary evangelicalism and the degree to which it links this evangelicalism to modernity.

Wells' approach to the issue is a function of his unique preparation and orientation. Wells is primarily a historian who taught in the field of church history before moving into the field of theology. This background is revealed by the fact that he generally does theology on the model of historical theology. His treatment of Christology, for example, is largely historical in orientation.[1] He frequently appears uncomfortable with the methodology and perspectives of philosophy. Thus, he chooses to deal with the issues of modernization from a historical and social science perspective. His way of introducing the whole subject of the changes that have taken place in introducing what he calls "Our Time" is to trace the history of a small town (Wenham, Massachusetts) from the mid-nineteenth century to the present, noting the alterations that have occurred.

Wells feels that too much emphasis has sometimes been placed on the purely ideological factors, the philosophy of a day or a movement. He faults Thomas Oden, for example, for focusing too exclusively on modernity in its intellectual dimension, especially as that

---

1. David F. Wells, *The Person of Christ: A Biblical and Historical Analysis of the Incarnation* (Westchester, Ill.: Crossway, 1984).

23

centers in the Enlightenment. He says of this approach which views modernity only in terms of ideas, that "it fails to understand the ways in which the social environment shapes consciousness and in turn produces a set of ideas that are matched in the environment."[2] This judgment is strengthened by his apparent endorsement of the sociology of knowledge: the idea "that the external social environment provides the explanation of internal consciousness, that the way we think is a product of the society in which we live."[3]

The Description of Modernity

With this qualification in mind, we will be better able to understand Wells' preliminary analysis of modernity, as depicted in the first two chapters of *No Place for Truth*. He asserts that somewhere between the middle of the nineteenth century and the middle of the twentieth century lies a great historical divide. The period before that could be called the Age of the West; the new period he calls simply Our Time. On the other side of that line, Europe was the center of the world, politically and economically; now America is. In the earlier period, there was a sense in which Judeo-Christian values were at the center of culture, even if they were not believed in personally. Now, however, there is no such set of values. Rather, they have been displaced and replaced by a loose set of psychological attitudes, which are now referred to as modernity.[4] This new period, Our Time, is not restricted by geography. It is not the civilization of any one group of people, in any one place. It is not political in nature. The soil from which it springs is that which capitalism and democracy produce, and it especially depends on technology and urbanization. But it may be found virtually anywhere that the requisite conditions are present.[5]

The inauguration of this civilization has been quite different in many ways from that of preceding cultures, which often came into ascendency through military or political conquest. That is not true of this period, however. Its ascendency has come about rather quietly, and in this sense it is the most benign civilization. Yet, despite

2. David F. Wells, *No Place for Truth: Or Whatever Happened to Evangelical Theology?* (Grand Rapids: Eerdmans, 1993), p. 63, n. 8.
3. Ibid., p. 72.
4. Ibid., pp. 53–54.
5. Ibid., p. 54.

the lack of violent transition, this period represents, just as genuinely as did earlier new cultures, a definite new culture, which breaks as sharply from what has preceded it as did any of those other, earlier, cultures. This culture is not simply contiguous with the preceding culture, but is continuous with it. Indeed, at times they seem almost indistinguishable from one another. And the later builds on the accomplishments of the earlier.[6]

What we are seeing is the decline of the West. While there were voices anticipating this decline in the nineteenth century, in the twentieth century this note has become much more common. What we see, side by side, are elements of decay and elements of renewal. The former tend to be regarded with concern by those of an Enlightenment orientation, for whom progress is always positive. Those who operate from a Judeo-Christian set of values, on the other hand, see in dissolution the first steps toward the realistic appraisal without which renewal is not possible.[7]

The Enlightenment world that has characterized much of modernity was an optimistic one. It was based on a strong confidence in human reason and its ability to solve humanity's problems unaided. This confidence, in turn, was based on an illusion, however, according to Wells—an illusion that an impersonal force was at work in the world promoting only the ends that the Enlightenment envisioned. This has not proven to be the case, however. For the fruits of this Enlightenment have been far from positive in many cases. Violence is present in our society in many forms. The powerful run roughshod over the weak. Many of the unborn never have an opportunity to live. Industry pollutes the earth. The elderly are encouraged to die and make room for those coming after them.[8]

The specific ideologies of the Enlightenment have promised much, but have failed to deliver on these promises. Darwinism, once it moved beyond the realm of the biological, has not produced the anticipated progress. In politics, both fascists and communists promised a new humanity, but this has not been forthcoming. The liberation from repression that Freudianism preached has not brought human freedom and wholeness. Similarly, the philosophical hope that the Absolute would move on to higher levels of civilization, the

6. Ibid., p. 55.
7. Ibid., pp. 55–57.
8. Ibid., p. 58.

hope of both Catholic and Protestant modernists for a society spiritually transformed, and the Victorian expectation that humanity was getting better and better in every way, were all alike disappointed.[9]

Despite this failure of the Enlightenment to remake human life, the premise on which the entire project was built does not die. That premise is freedom of all kinds: from God, from authority, from the past, from evil. Wells asks how this belief can continue in light of the incongruity of the results with the promises. He concludes that since contemporary persons are not self-consciously utopian, this belief is not based on intellectual reasons, but on the experience of science. Because science has been so successful in conquering disease, discomfort, and distance, there is an aura of immortality about it, and that on which it is based, namely, the belief in progress. There is no inherent connection between the ability to make better things and the ability to make better selves, yet the former seems to produce the expectation of the latter.[10]

Indeed, it is belief in the ability to move from one level of achievement to another that lies behind the constant desire to be *post-*. So we speak of being *post-*Puritan, *post-*Christian, *post-*modern, *post-*Vietnam, *post-*Watergate, and *post-*Cold War. Wells observes that while it is understandable that our society would want to leave behind these other experiences in favor of what it deems to be superior to them, it seems strange that people today would want to put behind the modernity that has made us what we are. Beyond that, however, Wells raises the question of whether it really is possible to move beyond the modern. This points up the different ways in which the word *modern* is used.[11]

As an intellectual phenomenon, the modern world began with the Enlightenment and its attempt to account for all of reality within the bounds of natural reason. It rejected external authority and placed the human at the center of reality. That project has ended in failure, however. In philosophy, for example, increasingly the human interpreter has come to have nothing to say. Not only does philosophy not consider itself capable of constructing great worldviews or synoptic visions encompassing the whole of reality. It now has given up its older belief that there is such a thing as truth and that it can be

9. Ibid., pp. 58–59.
10. Ibid.
11. Ibid., p. 60.

discovered. Philosophy's endeavor now is primarily pragmatic, and, in the view of Richard Rorty, therapeutic.[12]

If the modern world is dead or dying intellectually, however, the interesting and even striking fact is that just as this was happening, it was being born in its sociological form. While this is difficult to date with precision, Wells suggests that this transition to Our Time should be located somewhere in the last quarter of the nineteenth century.[13]

The juxtaposition of these two worlds, that which is modern in the intellectual sense and that which is modern in the cultural sense, is what produces the sometimes confusing contemporary picture. In the earlier period, intellectuals exerted a powerful influence on the world. The Enlightenment was launched by philosophers, and their ideas produced significant political changes in the world. In Our Time, however, ideas do not really count. Wells says:

> What shapes the modern world is not powerful minds but powerful forces, not philosophy but urbanization, capitalism, and technology. As the older quest for truth has collapsed, intellectual life has increasingly become little more than a gloss on the processes of modernization. Intellectuals merely serve as mirrors, reflecting what is taking place within society. They are post-modern in the sense that they are often disillusioned with the emptiness of the old Enlightenment ideals, but they are entirely modern in that they reflect the values of the impersonal processes of modernization.[14]

Here, then, is the ambiguity that we noted above: that many intellectuals are simultaneously modern and postmodern. Because they are modern sociologically, they believe in progress, in transcending the past, and thus are postmodern intellectually: "They are modern because they have to be postmodern."[15] Actually, if we have correctly understood what Wells has said to this point, this statement, since it is epistemologically correct but logically incorrect, is misleading. It is the fact that they are sociologically modern that results in the necessity of their being postmodern intellectually, not the reverse. But the fact that they find it necessary to be

12. Ibid., p. 60.
13. Ibid., p. 61.
14. Ibid.
15. Ibid.

27

postmodern intellectually is what reveals to us that they are modern sociologically.

As recent as this postmodernism claims to be, it is actually a continuation of various antimodernisms that appeared between 1880 and 1920. Those were protests against the overcivilized world, and a seeking for refuge in the simple life, quaint mind cures, and arts and crafts. That approach, however, did not see itself as going beyond modernity, but as standing out of its way.[16]

The Rise of Postmodernism

The current dissatisfaction with modernity, intellectually, has appeared in a wide variety of disciplines. One of the first was architecture, where modernism had attempted to develop a homogenized style that broke with the past and its indigenized designs by attempting to universalize, to belong everywhere because it did not belong anywhere in particular. Postmodern architecture broke with this by having many styles, reflecting interests of both the past and the present. It is one expression of our multiculturalism. But because it is not driven by any hard ideology, as was modernism, in its eclecticism it really does not have any definite purpose at all.[17]

In the old Enlightenment belief, there was confidence in the possibility of rational, objective scholarship. This has been rejected by postmodernism, intellectually. In the absence of any assent to a body of universal truth, even those conclusions that are presumably objectively discovered by scholars are seen to be only results of these scholars' interests and dispositions. Given the belief in relativism, there is great difficulty in insisting on the universal validity of one's findings. Even science, thought of as the paragon of objectivity and rationality by the modernists, is seen not to be exempt from this relativizing influence. Thomas Kuhn has shown that what scientists observe is very much affected by their anticipation of what they are looking for and what they consider possible. In literature, deconstruction holds that words do not have any meaning in themselves. They mean only what we want them to mean.[18] These same phenomena can also be seen in postmodern theology.

16. Ibid., pp. 61–62.
17. Ibid., pp. 64–65.
18. Ibid., p. 65.

Wells asserts, however, that the relationship between the modern and the postmodern is more complex than we sometimes recognize and acknowledge. The very fact that we insist on being postmodern, rather than merely antimodern, indicates a desire to transcend the recent past, which in turn reflects belief in progress. And this in itself is a clearly modern conception. Thus, even postmodernism has not fully freed itself from modernism. America, he contends, loves optimists and is impatient with naysayers. It is not merely that the arguments of those who think that the basis for hope for a better future is gone are wrong. Rather, they are offensive, for they violate a fundamental element of the American creed.[19]

Wells now turns to a discussion of this modernity that has come to pass. As observed earlier, he holds that the external social environment is the cause of the ways of thinking. In many respects, the shift from the Age of the West to Our Time has been a shift from the European to the American Age. The previous age was the great period of colonization, in which the European nations took the lead. Two World Wars wounded Europe and dismantled its empire, shifting the power to America.[20]

The changes should not be thought of as primarily political, however. Rather, they have come from a series of stunning inventions: "They have capitalized on each other and accidentally produced, in their human beneficiaries, new ways of looking at life, new values, new relationships to the society at large, new priorities, new horizons—in short, a new civilization."[21] This inventive outburst has been fueled by the Industrial Revolution, and has resulted in the organization of society into cities. The amazing thing about this development is that it has followed virtually the same path around the world, without regard for indigenous factors. The world civilization that is coming into being is technological and urban in nature, not national and cultural.[22]

Wells proposes to discuss and explain this change using two sets of concepts: modernization and modernity, and secularization and secularity. In each case, however, the former member of the couplet is to be thought of as primary and the latter as derivative. Modernity

19. Ibid., p. 67.
20. Ibid., pp. 68–69.
21. Ibid., p. 70.
22. Ibid.

is the consequence of modernization, while secularity is the consequence of secularization.[23]

By modernization, Wells means the process by which, for the sake of manufacturing and commerce, our society is organized into cities. This process results in the rise of modernity's values. He says, "In this context, the term *modernity* refers to the public environment created largely by urbanization, the moral etiquette, style of thought, and relationships of which are shaped by the large, impersonal structures that fill it."[24]

The effect of this modernization is to create two separated spheres, the public and the private. The one world is defined by personal relations, and is made up of small, insulated islands of home, family, and personal friends. The other is defined by the functions within the capitalistic machine. In this great system of production and distribution, persons are valued not for who they are or what they believe or hold as values, but for what they do. In this realm, in fact, personal relations may actually be a hindrance, since much efficiency depends on being impersonal. This anonymity also works against accountability. The worker is disengaged from any sense of responsibility for the product manufactured, any accountability to the ultimate consumer of the product.[25]

This urbanized modern workplace not only undercuts accountability, but it also has a similar effect on the cogency of religious belief and morality. Because of the wide range of worldview, cultural and ethnic difference, and personal values found in such close proximity, the values of each inhabitant have to be reduced to the lowest common denominator in order to eliminate antagonisms among the competing views. And when the public life is divested from the private world, it becomes connected instead to the machinery of the technological age. There also is a strong orientation to the future, as persons are "forced to anticipate and adapt to the oncoming change."[26]

In this modern society, the centers of culture have nothing to do with geography. Rather, they are involved with "a number of large, interlocking systems that form the structure of society." These are, for example, the economy; the political government (world, federal,

23. Ibid., p. 72.
24. Ibid., p. 74.
25. Ibid., pp. 74–75.
26. Ibid., pp. 75–76.

and state); the universities that generate and disseminate knowledge; and the mass media, which do the same for the images by which we understand ourselves. Although often not conscious of it, the persons within the society obtain "a sense of what is right and wrong, what is important and what is not" from these systems.[27]

The relationship that Wells has described between modernization and modernity is also found between secularization and secularism. In the final analysis, Wells concludes that secularization is almost a synonym for modernization. It is that aspect of modernization that produces the values of secularism, by which he means "the restructuring of thought and life to accommodate the absence or irrelevancy of God."[28]

Wells' concluding observation on the world cliché culture, as he calls it, is to say that what is novel about Our Time is not that it is modern. Rather, its novelty lies in three other considerations.

First, the modern consciousness is being shaped by a *world* civilization. It is not just the culture of one segment of the world, but of the whole. Second is the influence of the mass media as channels for the values of modernity. This is so invasive and pervasive as to give an intensity to the experience of modernity never before seen. Third, we are now seeing experimentation with and adoption of the values of modernity on an unprecedented scale.[29]

Religion's Response

These developments affect all persons, Christians and unbelievers alike. They have great power to shape the consciousness of those within society. In so doing, they have created an atmosphere in which unbelief seems natural and belief seems odd. Yet the church seems blissfully unaware of this condition, like the proverbial frog in the kettle. While this is a time of great peril, Wells believes that it is also a time of great opportunity. In the providence of God, times of reformation in the church's life frequently come out of times of disorder and chaos. God often tears down before he builds up, and this may be one of these times.[30]

27. Ibid., p. 77.
28. Ibid., p. 87.
29. Ibid., pp. 89–90.
30. Ibid., p. 91.

Unfortunately, religion, evangelical Christianity in particular, is not responding very well to this challenge, in Wells' judgment. He opened *No Place for Truth* with an account of the first day of his systematic theology course, in which a student complained after class about having to take systematic theology, which so obviously had no bearing on his future ministry. This sets the discussion of the entire book. Wells points out that theology has generally been comprised of three elements. The confessional element is the body of beliefs the church has inherited and holds, which crystallizes into doctrine. The reflective element is the church's endeavor to understand the meaning of being the recipient of God's Word in the present age. This in turn must proceed down three avenues. It must be biblical theology, covering the whole of Scripture and establishing the connections among the different parts. It must be historical theology, surveying the history of God's working in the church in the past. This will give the church the ballast necessary to assimilate the spiritual benefits of the past and to relativize the present with its pretentiousness. It must also be contemporary theology (although Wells does not use these terms), relating the content of the confession to what a given period considers normative. The third element is the cultivation of a set of virtues grounded in the first two elements. It is a matter of the church obtaining the wisdom that comes from basing its practice on its beliefs.[31]

The evangelical church has, however, been strongly influenced by the forces of modernization and has done poorly at carrying out these tasks of theology. Wells says, "As the nostrums of the therapeutic age supplant confession, and as preaching is psychologized, the meaning of Christian faith becomes privatized. At a single stroke, confession is eviscerated and reflection reduced mainly to thought about one's self." The pastor seeks to pattern the pastoral office and function in terms of the two roles that the culture most admires: the manager and the therapist. This is what theology is reduced to: reflection in the academy and practice in the church.[32]

One consequence of this modernization is that the church, including evangelicalism, is departing from what the church has historically been. Wells says, "In eviscerating theology in this way, by substituting for its defining, confessional center a new set of principles

31. Ibid., pp. 98–100.
32. Ibid., p. 101.

32

(if they can appropriately be called that), evangelicals are moving ever closer to the point at which they will no longer meaningfully be able to speak of themselves as historic Protestants."[33] He supports this claim by demonstrating that the apostolic message was very strongly based on the type of endeavor he has described as theology. The apostles, he asserts, declared the facts about Christ, interpreted those facts, and then applied them to the Christian life. It was this apostolic teaching that became the defining mark of a Christian: to be a believer meant to believe what the apostles taught. And the apostles did not simply teach doctrine. They insisted on its preservation and defense. It was the faith "once for all delivered," and was the only ground of hope. Nor was this a bare credal orthodoxy. Paul, for example, on numerous occasions, made clear the connection of belief and practice. But love and obedience could not be substituted for doctrinal belief. Rather, they were the expression of it and the demonstration of its genuineness.[34]

What amazes Wells is the argument by the World Council of Churches, implicitly backed by the Second Vatican Council, that because of today's pluralism, it is no longer possible to cling to the exclusiveness of the apostolic confession. Actually, the world in which the apostles lived and preached was more pluralistic than any other age until the present. While their world was small and ours is not, there is another very important difference between them and us, together with an important consequence:

> Theirs, however, was a cauldron of conflicting religious claims within which the Christian faith would have remained tiny but for one fact: the first Christians knew that their faith was absolutely true, that it could brook no rivals, and so they sought no compromises. That was the kind of integrity that God, the Holy Spirit, blessed and used in the ancient world in spreading the knowledge of Christ. We today are not so commonly persuaded or, I dare say, not so commonly blessed. Even among those who seek to guide the Church in its belief, many are of the mind that Christian faith is only relatively true, or they think, against every precept and example that we have in the New Testament, that Christ can be "encountered" in other religions—religions that they view not as rivals but as "interpretations" with which accommodation should be sought. What would have happened over the

33. Ibid., pp. 101–2.
34. Ibid., pp. 102–4.

ages, one wonders, if more of the Church's leaders had been similarly persuaded?[35]

The Disappearance of Evangelical Theology

Wells contends that theology is disappearing from evangelicalism. This may seem strange, since surveys indicate a strong continued belief in and commitment to the doctrines of historic Christianity. Yet, Wells contends, theology is disappearing because those beliefs have been pushed to the periphery, where their power to define what evangelical life should be has been lost. This disappearance means two things. On the one hand, the several aspects of theology have been broken apart. They are now engaged in, respectively, by biblical scholars; philosophers, historians, and sociologists; and the theoreticians of practice. Second, the articles of belief are no longer at the center of the life of evangelicals and evangelicalism. Instead, there is a vacuum, into which modernity is pouring. The result is that for the first time there is a faith that is not defining itself theologically.[36]

This disappearance of theology can be seen in two realms: the actual life of evangelicals and evangelical ministry. Evangelical piety has become very internalized, very privatized, a development that reflects the broader psychology of our day. At one time happiness was considered by evangelicals to be a by-product of right behavior. Now happiness has become the main goal of concern and activity. This experience of feeling good has increasingly become the object of much evangelical activity. This has enabled it to be very successful, for the consumer mentality simply is not hospitable to the habits of reflection and judgment required to frame and defend orthodox belief.[37] Wells shows the parallels between the message of Robert Schuller and that of Harry Emerson Fosdick. He says that the psychologizing of life undercuts historic Christianity at three points: (1) it assumes the perfectibility of human nature, contrary to the Christian gospel; (2) it undermines the desire and capacity to think, thus making theology impossible; (3) it severs interest in the outside world, sacrificing culture for self.[38]

Not only the understanding of the nature of evangelicalism but the understanding of ministry has been corrupted by modernization.

35. Ibid., p. 104.
36. Ibid., p. 109.
37. Ibid., pp. 171–73.
38. Ibid., pp. 178–84.

Two roles that are highly admired in our society have become the models that ministers now tend to adopt: the psychologist and the manager. Thus, preaching, even in evangelical pulpits, tends to be therapeutic, and the pastor is seen as the CEO of a corporation, responsible for its efficiency and growth.[39] This is in keeping with Wells' contrast between two types of ministry—one theologically based, the other professional in orientation. In the latter, one's occupation has become a career, in which advancing to larger, more financially rewarding, and more prestigious positions is the goal. Wells describes in considerable detail the process by which this has happened, and the present status of ministry and of the church.[40]

The new style of ministry is not actually one that enables the laity. In fact, Wells refers to the second type of clergy as the "new disablers." The result of their ministry is to create what Stanley Hauerwas and William Willimon have termed practical atheism: "It is an atheism that reduces the Church to nothing more than the services it offers or the good feelings the minister can generate. In other words, where professionalization is at work, there the ministry will typically be deprived of its transcendence and reduced to little more than a helping profession." It has produced a kind of sentimentality "that wants to listen without judging, that has opinions but little interest in truth, that is sympathetic but has no passion for that which is right. It is under this guise of piety—indeed, of professionalization— that pastoral unbelief lives out its life."[41]

Wells documents this contention from an examination of the nature of contemporary preaching as revealed by sermons published in two journals, *Preaching* and *Pulpit Digest*. He finds that less than 50 percent of these were explicitly biblical, and 14 percent were not discernibly biblical at all. Beyond that, he concludes that 80 percent were anthropocentric, that is, God and his will were not really at the center of considerations regarding the life of faith.[42] If Christians, evangelicals included, hold a faith in which modernity is at the center, in which they believe correct theology but it is detached from considerations of how they live, it is not surprising, for in a very real sense they are simply reflecting the pulpit.

39. Ibid., pp. 112–14.
40. Ibid., pp. 218–45.
41. Ibid., pp. 248–49.
42. Ibid., pp. 251–52.

Solutions

Wells has given considerable space to describing and analyzing the nature of modernity and its influence on evangelical thought and life. At times, this description becomes quite repetitious. If he is right, the situation is very serious for Christianity, the very nature and existence of which is at stake here. What does he propose as the response and solution to this vexing situation?

Basically, what Wells is calling for is a return to biblical truth—not only to its content, but to the very concept of truth. The Old Testament prophets and New Testament apostles had a certainty that contrasts sharply with modernity's outlook. They were convinced that the revelation that they had received from God and proclaimed was true in an absolute sense. It was not just true for them or true in their time alone. It was true "universally, absolutely, and enduringly."[43]

Wells is aware that this conception of truth is regarded by moderns as untenable. He advances three reasons moderns cite in defense of the position that we can no longer hold to absolute truth as those ancients did.

The first is often more implicitly assumed than argued per se. It is the idea that we have progressed to the point where we can no longer turn back to that older way of thinking. What is culturally older is considered to be of less value. While this was earlier based on Darwinism and the philosophy that stemmed from it, it has more recently been related to technology.[44]

Second, there is the contention that it simply is not possible to slip back into the ancient or biblical worldview, the way one would take off a garment and replace it with another. Worldviews are tied to the psychology and experiences of a given age, and ours is modern. While the argument of New Testament scholar Rudolf Bultmann along these lines is now considered obsolete, this belief seems to linger.[45]

Third, we now face religious pluralism and a bewildering array of claims to truth. It is therefore no longer possible to believe simplistically, as did the biblical writers, in an unqualified view of truth.[46]

43. Ibid., pp. 259–60.
44. Ibid., pp. 260–61.
45. Ibid., p. 261.
46. Ibid.

Wells responds to each of these contentions, arguing that they need not deter us from holding a biblical understanding of truth. First, to hold the view of the progress of the human spirit in view of the atrocities of this century requires a greater credulity than to believe the biblical writers.[47]

Second, from the fact of contemporary experience, it does not follow that we must simply acquiesce in this view. Experience is to be interpreted, and it certainly has not been shown that we have lost our freedom to accept or reject beliefs. If beliefs were strictly determined, what would be the point of writing books to persuade someone on any subject, including this one?[48]

Third, while religious pluralism in our time has reached a magnitude previously unequaled, it is quite remarkable to hear the claim that this requires giving up the uniqueness of Christianity. Wells says, "Had this been the necessary consequence of encountering a multitude of other religions, Moses, Isaiah, Jesus, and Paul would have given up biblical faith long before it became fashionable in Our Time to do so."[49]

Wells contrasts paganism with biblical Christianity, especially in terms of its view of truth. The pagan view involved the following ideas, each of which has echoes in the present:[50]

1. The gods could be known from nature, though to a limited extent.
2. Pagans proceeded from their experience to understand the supernatural.
3. The supernatural realm was neither stable nor predictable.
4. The pagan gods were sexual, so that the religious practice related to them had sexual overtones as well.
5. Pagans had no moral absolutes.
6. History had no real values for the pagans. They frequently considered history to be cyclical. They relied on their experience of the present.

47. Ibid.
48. Ibid., pp. 261–62.
49. Ibid., pp. 263–64.
50. Ibid., pp. 267–68.

Biblical Christianity, on the other hand, had very different ideas about history and truth:[51]

1. Biblical narrative works itself out in history.
2. The meaning of that history is present within it, and yet must be supplied by God.
3. The meaning of the biblical narrative can only be known at its completion. Eschatology is therefore very important.

In the final analysis, the major difference between the biblical understanding of truth and that of nonchristian views comes down to one important characteristic. For both the ancient pagan and the modern, truth is found within, in one's own private experience. For biblical Christianity, however, it is the obtaining of that which cannot be found within one's own experience. It is not simply a privatized set of beliefs that works for a person, and therefore is adopted pragmatically. It is the divinely revealed objective truth, that which is true for all persons at all times and places, reality as it is in itself, not as it appears to us.[52]

The solution to the problem, then, is for evangelical Christians to return to a concern for truth as objective knowledge of reality. Specifically, it is a matter of recapturing the understanding of persons, not as selves, but as human beings who stand before a holy God. Wells says, "If the Church can begin to find a place for theology by refocusing itself on the centrality of God, if it can rest upon his sufficiency, if it can recover its moral fiber, then it will have something to say to a world now drowning in modernity."[53]

Evaluation

Positive

This theology has a number of commendable features:

1. Wells has recognized that ideas and beliefs are not held in a vacuum, but are part of a given period, which has numer-

---

51. Ibid., p. 271.
52. Ibid., pp. 279–82.
53. Ibid., p. 301.

ous other cultural factors within it. The beliefs of a given time cannot really be divested from sociological factors, for example.

2. Wells has thoroughly documented the changes that have taken place in the culture, both outside and inside the church, in approximately the past century. It would be difficult to deny that a major change has taken place.

3. Wells has clearly demonstrated the difference between the biblical writers and preachers, and the outlook found outside the church and frequently also within the church, even the evangelical church, today.

4. Wells has correctly shown the connection between beliefs and practices, both in the teaching of the New Testament writers and in practical experience.

5. Wells has been courageous and willing to go against the stream in calling the church to renewal and reformation.

Negative

1. While seemingly endorsing the approach of the sociology of knowledge, Wells does not seem to realize that this also has a relativizing effect on the view he holds and the approach he recommends. Perhaps this is not simply the way things are, but a historically conditioned view.

2. Wells offers a thorough historical and social science analysis of the issues, but this is not matched by equally sophisticated philosophical analysis. For example, the problems raised by Kant are not given adequate treatment, either in terms of exposition or in terms of response.

3. A closely related problem is Well's failure to grapple with the epistemological issues raised by modernity. While he finds the biblical writers to be committed to a clearly objective view of truth, one modern response would be that he has read the Bible through his own objectivist presuppositions. This problem is not dealt with or even acknowledged. His response to modernity seems to assume the very issue that is in dispute. It is one thing to have absolute truth; quite another to understand it absolutely. This distinction appears to be missing from Wells' discussion.

4. It is not clear just what criteria Wells is employing in preserving elements from different intellectual periods. For example, he sounds at times as if he is advocating a return to premodernism. Yet he not only tolerates some features of modernity, including the technological, but embraces them. It is not apparent on what grounds he is making such a selection.

5. Perhaps the most serious negative factor is the lack of any real proposal for a solution of the contemporary church's problem. In *No Place for Truth*, Wells postpones treatment of this matter until the final chapter, and finally only the last five pages or less. He then wrote another book to deal with this lack, *God in the Wasteland*. This, however, tends to follow much the same pattern as the earlier book, again placing the solution largely in the final chapter. The analysis is heaped up to the point of becoming wearisome, but synthesis is extremely scarce.[54]

6. There are some indications that Wells has not escaped postmodernity as completely as he would have us think. His emphasis on the community approach to truth sounds strangely like the postmodern concern for community. In postmodernism, the community is introduced to provide some basis for objectivity against its inherent relativism. Wells does not articulate his position relative to this consideration.

7. Basically, the proposed solution is that evangelicalism must return to a belief in objective truth. How this is to be done is not really conveyed, however. It seems to be like telling a chemically dependent person simply to give up the use of drugs, cold turkey. But that is in a sense, not the answer, but the question, namely, "How do I do that?" What Wells offers corresponds in some ways to what is termed in ethics the ethical solution, or what should be done. What is lacking is the parallel to the practical solution, or how to bring about the desired ethical solution.

---

54. Wells' colleague, Richard Lints, displays the same tendency to overemphasize description and analysis, as well as to assume epistemological absolutism. See *The Fabric of Theology: A Prolegomenon to Evangelical Theology* (Grand Rapids: Eerdmans, 1993), as well as three unpublished papers presented at the meeting of the Midwest Region of the Evangelical Theological Society, St. Paul, Minn., March 16–17, 1995: "The Defining Moments of Evangelicalism"; "The Age That Cannot Name Itself"; and "Theology and the Many Faces of Modernity."

I have often asked myself just what I would have done had I been a pastor in the Deep South during the 1950s. Desiring to combat the evils perpetuated by the "separate but equal" policy, how would I have proceeded to lead the church to change? Too radical an insistence on immediate and total change might have been the means of guaranteeing that the effort would fail and that my chance to influence the congregation would be lost. Just how does the pastor who agrees with Wells, but does not have the sort of tenure that a professor has, proceed to implement his objectives?

Wells begins his book with an anecdote about a first day in class. Because he had received poor marks on course evaluations for introducing courses, he made a special effort to show the value of theology. After class a student came and declared to him the impracticality of theology, and his frustration with that situation is apparent.[55] But what if there were several students like that, perhaps a majority of the class, and they claimed the right to help determine what the content of classes should be, even the relative emphasis to be given to academics and other aspects of seminary life? What if they held the power of determining the professor's salary, or even of terminating the professor, if they were displeased with him? This would seem to be a parallel to the situation a local pastor faces. There seems to be a lack of empathy on Wells' part for the dilemma of the pastor or other church leader.

55. *No Place for Truth*, pp. 1–4.

3

Back to the Future

Thomas Oden

It is possible to understand some theologians' beliefs and teachings independently of an understanding of their biographies. The ideas are valid or invalid, apart from the events of their lives. With others, however, the very meaning of the teachings is so closely related to their experiences that one cannot really grasp the former without examining the latter. This is true of such theologians as Martin Luther, Søren Kierkegaard, and Karl Barth. And it is surely true as well of Thomas C. Oden, Henry Anson Butz Professor of Theology and Ethics at the theology school of Drew University, Madison, New Jersey.

In some ways, Oden is actually something of a parable of the theological changes we are discussing. For to study the entire corpus of his writings is to discover two Thomas Odens: the modern Oden and the postmodern Oden. Here is a man whose faith and theology have undergone a major transformation over the past two decades. He has described at considerable length his earlier views and his current theological stance. He has recounted his exposure to and involvement with a number of current ideas and causes during his student days and his early days as a professor, and describes this role as that of a "movement theologian."[1] As early as age sixteen he joined the United World Federalists to promote world government. He was

1. This following description of the "movement theologian" is found in *After Modernity . . . What? Agenda for Theology* (Grand Rapids: Zondervan, 1990), pp. 27–28.

also deeply involved in ecumenical actitivity, attending the 1954 Evanston Assembly of the World Council of Churches and the 1966 Geneva World Conference on Church and Society. He was involved in the Civil Rights Movement as well, beginning at about age seventeen, including attendance at the 1953 NAACP Convention, and participation in numerous marches, sit-ins, and the like. A decade before the Vietnam War, he was a pacifist and thought of himself as a democratic socialist and theoretical Marxist. He was an active worker in Students for Democratic Action, the American Civil Liberties Union, and the women's rights movement. He was a staunch advocate of liberalized abortion and an opponent of conservative causes such as states' rights and military spending. In the late 1950s, he became enamored of existentialism, including the demythologization movement. He earned his Ph.D. at Yale University, where he studied especially with Richard Niebuhr and wrote his dissertation on Rudolf Bultmann, the great demythologizer.

Each decade found Oden with a new set of ideas to follow and a new cause to champion. In the 1960s, he became involved in the client-centered therapy movement, Transactional Analysis, the Gestalt therapy movement, and the T-Group movement. In the 1970s, he joined a society for the study of paranormal activity, taught a class in parapsychology, and studied such matters as biorhythm charts, astrology, tarot cards, and the like.

Gradually, questions were beginning to form in Oden's mind and soul. More than anything, these stemmed from an uneasiness with the abortion on demand movement.[2] He feels that he can date quite exactly his movement into his postmodern period. He was preparing to leave for a research year, which meant that he would have to be away from his personal library for the entire twelve-month period. He had to choose carefully which books he would ship, for if he did not, the shipping cost would be atrocious. As he painfully made his reductions in a series of rounds, he made an astonishing discovery: not one of the books on his final list was from the twentieth century. It was the earlier classics that he had come to rely on for his personal growth and being. He says:

> I learned something important about myself on that fateful day. It felt as though the second Christian millennium was already over for me

2. Ibid., pp. 28–29.

spiritually. It was as if it had burned itself out several years before its expected demise.

If I had to assign a date to my entrance into the 'post-modern' world (similar to the way the frontier revivalists used to speak of the exact day they were converted), I think it would be that day when I had to choose the books I most needed, and most certainly wanted with me, and discovered to my astonishment that if push came to shove I could do without the twentieth-century material altogether, but that I could not seem to do without Hippolytus, Thomas Aquinas, Nicholas of Cusa, *Theologia Germanica,* Maimonides, Pascal, and Kierkegaard.[3]

This "reversal," as Oden terms it, has been progressively unfolding for approximately the past two decades. A comparison of the writings of the earlier Oden with those of the later Oden reveals a striking contrast. He speaks of the narrowness of his earlier academic and ecclesiastical acquaintances. He had restricted his conversations almost entirely to university colleagues and liberal churchmen, and was delighted to discover the quality of scholarship among Protestant evangelicals and Catholics.[4] It is this later Oden whose thought we examine in this chapter.

Characterization of Modernity

Modernity, as Oden uses it, has several meanings. It can be dated quite precisely, in his judgment. It is "the period, the ideology, and the malaise of the time from 1789 to 1989, from the Bastille to the Berlin Wall."[5] It is, however, to be thought of as less a period than "a conceptual place, an ideological tone . . . an attitude."[6] It was not until the nineteenth century that it began to expand from the intellectual intelligentsia to the common people, and by the twentieth century, moral attitudes that were considered objectionable and disreputable in earlier periods had become part of the *Zeitgeist*.[7]

Oden acknowledges that the beginning point of the modern period is dated variously by different commentators. While he dates it

3. Ibid., p. 25.
4. Ibid., p. 29.
5. Thomas C. Oden, "The Death of Modernity and Postmodern Evangelical Spirituality," in *The Challenge of Postmodernism: An Evangelical Engagement*, ed. David S. Dockery (Wheaton, Ill.: Victor, 1995), p. 20.
6. *After Modernity . . . What?* p. 44.
7. Ibid.

from the time of the French Revolution, specifically the storming of the Bastille (1789), some date it from the beginning of printing (about 1450), or from some point in between, such as Descartes or the social contract.[8] Its end can also be rather precisely located, with the fall of the Berlin Wall in 1989.[9] Its meaning comes from the Latin words *modernus* (of the present time) and *modus* (measure). Thus, "something is *mod*ified if it is changed, varied, or given a new form. A mode is a prevailing style or current fashion."[10] As applied to such fields as art, music, furniture, and literature, it refers to what is current as contrasted with the traditional. There is, in modernity, a pretense that what is not modern, what has gone before, "is not adequate, is antiquated, and therefore is to be thrown away."[11] Although Oden does not mention it, this is the idea behind the concept that something is "outmoded." Its mode has passed, being supplanted by a new mode.

Oden elaborates his definition by describing three distinct strata of meanings. These are like three concentric circles in a target:[12]

1. There is an overarching intellectual ideology of the historical period designated as modernism. The assumptions of the French Enlightenment, together with German idealism and British empiricism, combine to form a worldview that has dominated the modern period, especially among the intellectual elite.[13] Its key general features are moral relativism, narcissistic hedonism, naturalistic reductionism, and autonomous individualism.

2. There is a mentality that assumes the superiority of chronologically recent ways of knowing as contrasted with anything premodern. Indeed, this is not thought of as an assumption, but as a self-evident truth. This Oden also describes as the chauvinism of modernity.

3. Finally, the inner circle, the bull's-eye, is modernity in the sense of "the *later-stage deterioration of both* of the preceding viewpoints."[14] While this deterioration has been accelerating during the last half of this century, it has become especially rapid and dramatic during the past three decades.

8. Ibid., p. 46.
9. "Death of Modernity," p. 20.
10. *After Modernity*, p. 44.
11. Ibid., p. 45.
12. Ibid., pp. 46–47.
13. "Death of Modernity," p. 24.
14. Ibid., p. 45.

There are some especially revealing features of the modern consciousness. A very conspicuous one is the rhetoric of unrestrained individual freedom. There is a strong desire to be free from all restrictions, all traditions, all social parenting. These are thought to be dehumanizing. Modernity thinks, "If we were only free from *x* or *y*, then we could truly be ourselves."[15] This is the push for self-actualization, self-realization, of which we hear so much. It shows itself in many ways, one of which is the Freudian reaction against any sort of sexual repression. Yet it is not just in the psychoanalytic theories that such freedom is glorified, but in politics, modern theater, film, the arts, and popular culture. It is an abstract kind of freedom, because it is abstracted or taken away from its matrix of social accountability. This is freedom without its concomitant responsibility. It is freedom of an individual sort. Instead of covenant responsibility, there is only subjective self-expression, which Oden terms "inordinate, hedonic self-assertiveness."[16]

This narcissistic hedonism especially makes an idol of one's sensuality, body, and immediate pleasures. The central value is making "me" feel good right now; all other values are demoted in favor of this. Oden says, "Narcissistic hedonism is that orientation to life that fixates upon my pleasure and regards that fixation as the best one can expect of the self."[17] Its pervasiveness is almost institutionalized: "This hedonic idolatry looms in living color in the network tube in what is advertised as family entertainment, but which turns out to be fixated on sex and violence."[18]

Closely related to this is the moral relativism of modernity. All human moral values are historically conditioned. They are contingent on "the changing social and psychological determinants of human cultures."[19] On this understanding, there is no basis for criticism of the norms of another, no normative way to judge norms. Thus, when dealing with what traditional societies regarded as legitimated values, modernity translates these into descriptions of the norms held by others. This act of safety amounts to a debunking of all norms, however, according to Oden.[20] There is simply a tolera-

15. *After Modernity*, p. 47.
16. Ibid.
17. "Death of Modernity," p. 28.
18. Ibid., p. 29.
19. Ibid.
20. *After Modernity*, p. 80.

tion of the moral norms of others. One must not impose one's own opinions or moral convictions on others.[21]

Another prominent feature of this modern mentality is chronological chauvinism. This has several features, which Oden characterizes as "a predisposed contempt for premodern ideas, a vague boredom in the face of the heroic struggles of primitive and historical human communities, a diffuse disrespect for the intellectual, social, and moral achievements of previous periods."[22] A moment's reflection on the widespread current ignorance of history and disdain for the events of even fifty years ago will immediately lead us to recognize the phenomena of which Oden is writing. Some, of course, would contend that this is to be expected of any period, whose egocentricity would lead it to disrespect all other social norms and intellectual ideas. Such an objection is disproved by the fact that some other societies have great respect for earlier social structures and ideas and for the traditions of their ancestors.[23]

This sort of chauvinism has become pervasive in our time. In fact, Oden suggests that the words *new* and *change* have become "magic words." He asks the reader to perform an experiment by counting the number of times in ordinary conversation that *new* and *good* are used as synonyms, and conversely, to ask whether *change* is ever used pejoratively. The silent assumption is that the new is good and that change is always improvement. Academics, he claims, use more sophisticated words, like *emergent, innovative, revolutionary,* and *metamorphosis.* This is magic, and he recommends, as part of a postcritical consciousness, that one stop using *new* and *change* as magic words, that one just go "cold turkey" in this matter. Modernity also has its bad magic words: "Anything that looks 'old hat' or 'antiquated' or 'rigid' or 'traditional' will be subtly linked implicitly with evils to be avoided, vicious repressions that hold us down, powers of darkness. The adjectives abound—all with a stale smell: paleo-anything, medieval, obsolete, senile, elderly, bygone, extinct."[24]

Further, there is a strong rejection of parenting. This can be seen most clearly, of course, when an adolescent rebels against his or her

21. Thomas C. Oden, *Requiem: A Lament in Three Movements* (Nashville: Abingdon, 1995), p. 24.
22. *After Modernity*, pp. 47–50.
23. Ibid., p. 50.
24. Ibid., p. 42.

parents' teaching and control. It goes beyond that to rejection of so-cial parenting. Modernity rejects any sort of societal control or even influence as inherently repressive. There is no value seen in and no responsibility taken for nurturing social continuities or moral tradi-tion that carries on from one generation to another. The individual is believed to be more competent to reconstruct the human situation than any social tradition. Historical wisdom of all sorts is dis-regarded in favor of individual judgment. Oden acknowledges that in all generations the struggle of the adolescent to become indepen-dent is to be expected. In this case, however, it has become a total worldview, involving political ethics, psychological strategy, and in-terpersonal posture.[25] Although Oden does not discuss this phenom-enon specifically in terms of its relationship to the demographic phe-nomenon of the baby boomer generation, it can be seen that this accentuates the problem. Whereas in previous times the control of the mentality has tended to rest with the older generation and has been something that the newer generation has had to rebel against, in the case of the baby boomers, their sheer numbers meant that they have been able to establish their ideas and values and in effect impose them on the society.

Mentioned more briefly is naturalistic reductionism—the ten-dency to reduce all explanation of phenomena to natural causes, and to exclude by assumption anything that transcends the natural or even the material. This appears most clearly in connection with the historical method, where natural explanations must be found for all events and are the only sort of explanations accepted or even consid-ered.[26] Reductionism appears in the fact that empirical observation is so idolized that no other source of knowledge is really admitted. The only reliable form of knowing is found in laboratory experimen-tation and quantitative analysis. Here, "sex has become reduced to orgasm, persons to bodies, psychology to stimuli, economics to plan-ning mechanisms, and politics to machinery."[27] In such an atmo-sphere, orthodox Christianity is not really even admitted to the uni-versity. We may certainly understand in part the university's reluctance, based on recollection of specific abuses that orthodoxy has inflicted on various disciplines in the past, but it fails to recall the

25. Ibid., p. 50.
26. Ibid., pp. 124, 190.
27. "Death of Modernity," p. 29.

positive moments and positive contributions that classic Christianity has made.[28]

Postmodernity

In much popular parlance, the term *postmodern* is applied to movements that claim to represent the antithesis of the modern spirit. This, for example, is often used of the deconstructionism of Derridá and Foucault. This deconstructivistic literary criticism and the relativistic nihilism of someone like Richard Rorty is actually, in Oden's judgment, a despairing belief that the modern patterns will reduplicate endlessly. Whereas he earlier referred to this period and movement as late modernity, he now refers to it as "ultramodernity." Its representatives wrongly think of themselves as at the end of modern consciousness. Actually, however, "their philosophical commitments and value judgments show the very kind of relativism that characterizes ultramodern despair."[29] Oden contends that he used the term in 1969 in reference to spiritual wanderers who are looking for roots, and that this antedated Derridá and Foucault popularizing the term and the architectural word "shanghaiing" it. He believes that "the ideology of automatic progress has glazed their eyes."[30] He poses the question whether he should not simply abandon the word *postmodern,* since it has been so badly corrupted, but nonetheless insists on retaining it because of its descriptive value and rhetorical utility, and believes that those who have given a later spin to an earlier use of the word are the ones who should have to justify their use in the new meaning. Its descriptive value lies in the fact that "the logic of modernity requires something to follow it, even when the myth of modernity lives in denial of that possibility."[31]

The Death of Modernity

Oden contends that modernity in its ultramodern phase is actual terminal modernity. This is a terminally fragmenting modernity. In the past thirty years, "we have personally witnessed the rapid dissolution of what at the beginning of those thirty years seemed to be a

28. *After Modernity*, p. 190.
29. "Death of Modernity," p. 26.
30. *Requiem*, p. 117.
31. Ibid.; "Death of Modernity," pp. 26–27.

stable intellectual environment that we expected to last many centuries." Like watching the crash of a daredevil at a flying exhibition, we have, to our horror witnessed the disintegration of the worldview that had been in place for two hundred years. This is "the acute phase of rapidly deteriorating modernity."[32]

What has brought about this deterioration and what signals the death of modernity is a moral spinout, like the tailspin and crash of the flyer mentioned above. The moral fruits of the modern period have been borne, and they are proving to be a cataclysm. Oden says:

> The party is over for the hedonic sexual revolution of the period from the sexy sixties to the gay nineties. The party crasher is sexually transmitted diseases. We are now having to learn to live with the consequences of sexual, interpersonal, and familial wreckage to which narcissistic self-indulgence has led us. Its interpersonal fruits are friendlessness, dissaffection, divorce, drug abuse, and the despairing substitution of sexual experimentation for intimacy.[33]

Oden brings the microscope closer to examine in greater detail the effects of this collapse. These correspond to the four fallen idols, the four strains of terminal modernity.[34]

1. Autonomous individualism has led to "intergenerational conflict, sexual detachment, family decomposition, and societal havoc." Cut off from community, the lonely self has to seek meaning on its own. Cities, families, and politics of terminal modernity must now live with the consequences of this radical individualism. This individualism "has now come down to gun battles between eleven-year-old boys with flashing tennis shoes."[35]

2. Narcissistic hedonism, conducted in the absence of concern for anyone else, has borne its fruits in "a tangible hell, an anticipatory real damnation, as best symbolized by the actual recent history of sexuality."[36] It has led to a moral numbness or stupor. And it has led to real misery for others, who are harmed by the hedonistic pursuit of pleasure: "The fact that one person's narcissistic binge may turn into another's lifelong misery is evident from the shocking number

---

32. *Requiem*, p. 116.
33. Ibid.
34. "Death of Modernity," pp. 28–29.
35. *Requiem*, p. 118.
36. "Death of Modernity," p. 28.

of American babies being born suffering from their mother's drug addictions—currently averaging over 300,000 per year."[37]

3. Reductive naturalism, by its emphasis on empirical observation, has ignored any other proposed source of knowledge, including intuitive, personal, and revealed. In the search for natural finite material and efficient causes, however, it "denies freedom and abolishes all forms of purposeful antecedent and final causality, and thus misunderstands human accountability."[38]

4. Absolute moral relativism, by asserting normlessness uncritically and absolutely, has become a new kind of dogmatism. So, Oden says, "Terminal modernity is being forced to live with the disastrous social fallout of its own relativistic assumptions: moral anomie, the forgetfulness of final judgment beyond history, the reduction of all moral claims to a common denominator of mediocrity."[39]

In short, what has brought modernity to its demise has not been an elaborate intellectual refutation of its theoretical conceptions. It has been the consequences that have followed from that mentality. As Oden puts it,

> Not some theory but actual modern *history* is what is killing the ideology of modernity. I need only mention Auschwitz, Mylai, Solzhenitsyn's *Gulag Archipelago*, *Hustler* magazine, the assault statistics in public schools, the juvenile suicide rate, or the cocaine babies. All these point to the depth of the failure of modern consciousness. While modernity continues blandly to teach us that we are moving ever upward and onward, the actual history of late modernity is increasingly brutal, barbarian, and malignant. We see unfolding before our eyes the troubled, conflicted alliance between an optimistic evolutionary progressivism and regressive forms of nativist narcissistic hedonism.[40]

It is a practical failure of modernity that has brought about its doom. It is necessary to temper somewhat that statement: "It is best to state it modestly, even meekly: we are now entering into a historical phase in which the strengths of modern ideological motifs are rapidly diminishing, and whatever is to follow modernity is already

37. *Requiem*, p. 118.
38. Ibid.
39. "Death of Modernity," p. 29.
40. *After Modernity*, p. 51.

taking embryonic form."[41] The transition into the world that will follow modernity may take several decades, but it will come, and with it will come an age that is less enthusiastic about the conceptions of modernity that have proven to be illusions.[42]

What, then, can we expect in this postmodern era? As we already noted, Oden does not believe that what is frequently termed "postmodernism" should really be called that, since it shares, even in exaggerated form, the same assumptions of modernity. Rather, he is using the term initially in a nonideological sense. It is simply temporal, that which comes after the modern period. He says, "'Post' simply means after, following upon, later than. So postmodernity in our meaning is nothing more or less enigmatic than *what follows modernity*."[43]

In a very real sense, he seems to be saying that there is an opportunity to seize the initiative at this point and help determine what form this postmodernism will take. He is encouraged by the fact that evangelicalism has outlived the dissolution of modernity. A postmodern recovery of classical Christianity is taking place.

It is certain, in Oden's judgment, that the postmodern period will not belong to liberal Christianity. That movement has tied itself too closely to modernity, and is already suffering a decline along with that movement, a decline that will surely accelerate. That liberal form of Christianity, especially as represented in the theological seminaries of the so-called mainline denominations, does not possess the strength to capitalize on the opportunity available, as Oden has documented in his book, *Requiem*. Because liberal Christianity blindly bought into the belief that whatever is recent is automatically better than what is older, it did not bother to consult any premodern insights from Christianity. Indeed, there has come to be a harsh repression of anything antedating modernity.

For Oden, the type of Christianity that he has found satisfying following his disillusionment with modernity is classical orthodox Christianity. By that he means the consensual core of beliefs that has been held by a majority of the church throughout the span of its historical existence, embodied in such documents as the ecumenical creeds of the early centuries. It is this body of material, long over-

41. "Death of Modernity," p. 30
42. Ibid., p. 31.
43. Ibid., p. 25.

looked or ignored by mainline Christianity, that will prove to be a vital source of postmodern orthodoxy.[44]

Oden is emphatic in pointing out that postmodern does *not* mean antimodern. There are two reasons for this and two meanings of this statement. One is that it is unnecessary to oppose modernity, for it is dying. One need not be opposed to that which is already dead. Thus, the reaction of postmodern orthodoxy to modernity is not primarily anger or animosity, but, if anything, sadness. Its fundamental thesis is not that modernity is corrupt, but that it is defunct, obsolete, and antiquated.[45]

There is a second reason why this is not to be understood as antimodern. These are persons who have passed through modernity, who have experienced its strengths and its weaknesses and have learned from it. Oden is not advocating a simplistic, sentimental return to premodernism, as if there had never been a modernity. The achievements of modernity are not to be circumvented or short-circuited. The rebuilding from the crash of modernity is to be done using treasures both old and new. "These young people have been hardened by modernity to use the methods of modern inquiry (the methods of psychological analysis, sociological, political, historical analysis, scientific and literary analysis) to detoxify the illusions of modernity."[46] What makes such postmoderns "post" is that "they are no longer intimidated by the once dominant voices of what Oden terms 'mod rot.'" It appears that it is the narrow dogmas of Enlightenment thought, which ruled out certain great forgotten wisdoms, that must be rejected, so that those wisdoms may once again be considered and employed in building a new evangelicalism.[47]

What, then, is it that Oden is recommending? In part, it is a new voice for the Scriptures. This involves a considerable critique of biblical criticism as it has been practiced in the modern period. There is a legitimate use of critical methodology, and that should be retained as a useful means of assisting us in understanding the Bible's message. But modern critics often assume that criticism began in the modern period and that assumption is quite inaccurate. Critical-historical inquiry goes back more than a millennium before moder-

44. "So What Happens after Modernity," p. 398.
45. "Death of Modernity," p. 21.
46. Ibid.
47. Ibid.

nity. It grew out of classical Christianity, but it was lost in the scholasticism of the Middle Ages, only to be revived in the Renaissance.
Modern criticism, however, with its historical chauvinism, carries a
strong prejudice against anything premodern. This, Oden contends,
is not so much criticism as prejudice.[48]

Oden contends that we must engage in criticism of criticism, especially singling out form criticism for attack. He observes that form
critics engage in an activity with interesting similarities to psycho-
analysis. Psychoanalysts seek to get to deeper layers of unconscious
influence in the personality of their clients. Similarly, form criticism
looks for hidden layers of meaning in the text, of which the author
was not aware. Both endeavors are highly speculative in nature.
They claim to be scientific, but that claim is specious, for form critics
engage in little more than intuitive guessing, based on mere shreds of
evidence. Yet a system of tenure and "an elaborate apparatus of professional impression-management which has become deeply en-
sconced in departmental bureaucracies of German and American
universities for over half a century" protects the "hardened orthodoxy" of form criticism.[49] Oden is particularly critical of the "criterion of dissimilarity," which in effect requires that only those alleged
sayings of Jesus that can be shown not to have any parallel in Judaism or the Hellenic church can be considered authentic. Oden points
out that this is not the sort of procedure or standard of evidence followed in U.S. courts of law, where a person is considered innocent
until proven guilty. Nor is such a criterion ordinarily employed in literary criticism. If this were the case, then whenever Shakespeare used
a phrase found elsewhere, we would have to judge that this was not
authentically written by Shakespeare. Oden also points out that this
is not the way persons function in ordinary conversation. They do
not use only those words they uniquely possess. They draw on words
generally available in the culture, and these invariably have a long
history, nuances of meaning, and multiple associations.[50]

Underlying form criticism's methodology is a theory of development of the New Testament canon that assumes progression—from

48. *After Modernity*, p. 110. I have coined the term "chronocentrism" to refer to
this chauvinism, which often includes a tendency to act as if the postmodern period
will never be succeeded by a new period.
49. Ibid., p. 112.
50. Ibid., pp. 113–14.

an oral tradition; through Paul; the Synoptic Gospels; Hebrews, the Pastorals, and John; the end of the New Testament period—culminating in the complete depositum and formation of the canon. The assumption is that the earlier stages in this process are more reliable, the later ones less so. This, however, is a prejudicial assumption against the view of classical exegesis that the earlier phases of development were a fully adequate deposit, needing later phases to explicate and develop certain key themes within them.[51] Yet even on the basis of the principle of dissimilarity, what emerge as authentic sayings of Jesus still contain "the rudiments of classic Christian teaching—triunity and theandric union in the person of Christ."[52] Oden also examines the attempts to determine Jesus' self-understanding. He observes how difficult it is to determine from one's writings and speaking just what one thinks of oneself, even when dealing with a contemporary person, to say nothing of a historical figure.[53]

Oden further considers the critical view that there is a difference between the historical Jesus and the person proclaimed by the church. The difficulty is supposed to stem from the attribution by Paul to Jesus of ideas of him as Messiah or Son of God, which Jesus himself did not claim or believe. These ideas of Paul are supposed to have come from circles of hellenizing Judaism (Wrede) or a gnostic redeemer myth (Bultmann). Oden, however, sees in this a strong indication of the hubris of modern criticism. It is more plausible to hold the classic view that "no one other than the Christ of the synoptics could have inaugurated the messianic reign." The former view is based on the idea that the critics of the present time know more about Jesus than did Jesus himself or those who lived almost twenty centuries before us.[54]

Oden contends that the historical method employed by the modern critics contains modern assumptions, which are rigid and reductionistic and often biased against the idea that anything genuinely supernatural occurs. This involves the use of the methodology of the scientific laboratory, which studies objects, rather than that of the courtroom, which deals with persons and events. Even the courtroom methodology cannot be fully employed in investigating his-

51. Ibid., p. 115.
52. Ibid., pp. 116–17.
53. Ibid., pp. 117–18.
54. Ibid., pp. 118–20.

tory, however, for in the courtroom witnesses can be interrogated, which cannot be done with historical personages. The critics' offense is that of deciding in advance what evidence is acceptable. That assumption must be challenged.[55]

The problem with modern theology is that it has bought into the whole mentality of modernity, and thus suffers all the shortcomings that it possesses. It is empty and unable to save or offer any real hope for the world's needs. It has become so committed to a political agenda that it cannot really be of any help. It has, however, managed to capture the positions of control in old-line denominations, as well as the chairs in many seminaries, and exercises strong political control and veto power, by which it excludes genuine orthodox Christianity from those centers of influence.[56]

If exposing the presumption and intolerance of modernity as applied to the Christian faith is one major part of Oden's agenda, the other is the pursuit of paleo-orthodoxy. This awkward term is one Oden feels compelled to use because of his desire not to have this movement confused with neo-orthodoxy, which failed to present an adequate response to modernity. Those who advocated it either had not fully drunk deeply enough of modernity or tended to reject orthodox Christianity.[57] Nor does Oden wish to accept or return to fundamentalism, in the sense of the theology identified by the list of five fundamentals. Oden notes that each of these was concerned with a historical event, such as the virgin birth or the resurrection, rather than with the doctrinal meaning of those events, and that it neglected a number of other doctrines, such as sin, sanctification, and the church. He believes that this was because, together with liberalism, fundamentalism held the modern view that faith is based on objectively determinable, historical facts. It therefore had more in common with liberalism than it would be willing to admit. It was, in other words, strongly influenced by and representative of modernity.[58] What Oden is calling for is a return to the classical orthodoxy that has characterized Christianity throughout much of its history. There has been a consensus, represented in the Christian writings of the first millennium and found in ecumenical creeds (such as the Nicene, the

55. Ibid., pp. 124–26.
56. *Requiem*, pp. 34–41.
57. *After Modernity*, pp. 63–66.
58. Ibid., pp. 66–68.

Chalcedonian, etc.). Although this paleo-orthodoxy is returning to its premodern roots, it is not premodern but postmodern. It is the new spirituality that is emerging out of the failure of modernity.[59] Theologically, it is an attempt to speak of the God who has disclosed himself in history. Those events are "made known in Scripture, rigorously reflected upon by reason, and experienced personally through a living liturgical tradition."[60] But why the agenda of the first millennium? Oden recommends it "not because this period was intrinsically more exciting than other eras, or its advocates more brilliant, but because of its close adherence to apostolic faith and because a more complete ecumenical consensus was achieved in that period than in any other period since, a consensus that in fact has been subsequently affirmed by Protestant, Catholic, and Orthodox traditions."[61]

Evaluation

We have seen a bold approach to the issues of modernity and postmodernism. Is this an adequate and helpful treatment of our problem?

Positive

There is much about this approach to commend it.

1. It has a strong ring of authenticity. The genuineness of experience comes through clearly, with even a measure of pathos. Here is a genuinely postmodern person, who has drunk about as deeply as possible of the fountains of modernity as a theologian, and who has seen the futility of this approach. When Oden speaks, therefore, he clearly knows whereof he speaks. He cannot be accused of being merely a premodern or a fundamentalist. His testimony is more impressive than that of someone who has simply observed modernity from afar.

2. Oden has given an accurate description of modernity. Those of us who have encountered it in contemporary universities, have dialogued with living representatives of the movement, and have read their contemporary writings recognize well what he is describing. While one might wish for more documentation of the views he is dealing with, his analysis is profoundly insightful.

59. "Death," pp. 22–23.
60. *After Modernity*, p. 160.
61. Ibid., p. 161.

3. Oden has thoroughly and almost ruthlessly traced out the consequences of modernity. He has shown the end result of this mentality, something its advocates often have not been able or willing to do. He has given a sobering warning to those now within the ideology, or considering adopting it, regarding the end results of such a system.

4. Oden has laid bare the biases present within many old-line denominations, seminaries, and universities. The greater adeptness in political matters of modern persons has indeed enabled them to control the ideology of such schools, systematically excluding those of a more conservative bent. Tolerance is extended only to certain approved views. As one person put it, "Some people are more equal than others." The official line is that such persons are not scholarly, but as Oden discovered, in many cases, the scholarship and acuteness of insight of many conservatives exceed that of those in "liberated" positions. The only thing new about Political Correctness is that of late it has become visible in wider circles. For a long time there have been official orthodoxies in many university departments, and differing viewpoints are ignored. My undergraduate major in a state university, for example, was in a philosophy department that, with one exception, was populated exclusively by professors representing the logical positivist or analytical perspective. Similarly, the faculty of the psychology department in which I minored, were, to a person, behaviorists. Oden is to be admired for the courage and candor with which he has exposed the biases of these institutions.

Oden is in large part correct in terming what is often called postmodernism, "hypermodernism." For long before the breaking forth of what is popularly identified as postmodernism, many of the tendencies that he described were already present in modernity, especially within existentialism, where the individualism, narcissism, and hedonism were prominent.

6. Oden's criticism of much contemporary biblical criticism is right on target. The conclusions have in many cases been built into the methodology by the adoption, perhaps unconsciously, of an anti-supernaturalistic bias. The criteria utilized are both arbitrary and unrealistic in many cases. Hopefully, many conservative theology students and others will be able, because of Oden's critique, to resist the inappropriate conclusions of radical criticism.

7. Oden has correctly pointed out that critical study of the Bible is not something that began within the past 100 or 150 years. There was much in the earlier history of the church and theology that, without the modern presuppositions, was critical and very helpful in its unfolding of the meaning of the biblical text.

Negative

Despite these significant basic strengths, there are areas in Oden's proposal that are in need of further development.

1. Oden indicates that the postmodern is not to be antimodern. There is much of value within modernity that should be retained. There needs to be elaboration, however, of the criteria to be employed in deciding what should be retained and what should be discarded. He is quick to identify technological advances achieved by modernity for which we are to be grateful and which we should not hesitate to use. Beyond that, however, how do we decide? Oden sees values within biblical criticism, but does not tell us where we should draw the line. Is all criticism acceptable, so long as it does not exclude the supernatural or eliminate elements of the orthodox consensus? Further work here would be desirable.

2. To focus the previous point somewhat more sharply: Oden is proposing a postmodern orthodoxy, not simply a return to premodern thought. If this is to be done, however, then he must deal with some of the epistemological problems raised by modernity, which the orthodox of the first millennium of Christianity could not anticipate or deal with. For example, if one rejects the modern answers to the problems raised by Kant in his critiques, one must give some other answer. One cannot merely pretend that Kant never lived, thought, and wrote. Nor is it possible simply to dismiss Kant because he was modern. The question may well be answerable, but it must be answered. If not, one is in danger of simply perpetuating premodernism.

3. There is no real analysis and explanation of the existence simultaneously within modernity of strongly conflicting positions. For example, accompanying the strong individualism and egocentrism that stemmed from existentialism is the rational and even reductive empiricism of scientific modernity. Are these conflicting characteristics of the same mentality, or are they two different things? In other words, should one speak of moderni*ties?* This seems to be an unre-

solved question in Oden's thought. In part, he does not seem suffi-
ciently to credit the strongly antirational stream, especially in later
modernity.

4. Oden indicates that he personally accepts existentialism, especially that of Kierkegaard. Yet, at the same time, he rejects some of
the movements that drew on his thought, and that seemed to find inspiration there for their own variety of modernity. Even within theology, he rejects the efforts of Barth and Niebuhr as either insufficiently exposed to modernity or insufficiently appreciative of
orthodoxy. Both theologians, however, were strongly dependent on
Kierkegaard, and there are some very strong similarities between
their thought and his. Surely this paradox needs some resolution.

5. Oden faults fundamentalism for being too modern in many
ways, especially as revealed in its concern with the historical reality
of the virgin birth and the resurrection of Jesus, rather than their
doctrinal significance. He attributes this to fundamentalism's buy-
ing into the historicism of the nineteenth century. While this may
be true, at least in part, he does not seem to give adequate weight
to the fact that it was in this realm that the challenges from liberalism were coming. The fundamentalists most certainly had doctrines
of sin, sanctification, and the church, but it was the reality of the
deity of Christ that was under attack. Discussion of the doctrinal
significance of the virgin birth and resurrection was unimportant if
those did not actually occur. Perhaps this comment may indicate
that Oden has not broken completely free of his Bultmannian presuppositions.

6. This points up a bit of ambiguity in Oden's relationship to history and historical method. He seems to approve of Pannenberg's
use of history in his theology, yet that involves a conception of history which, although it carefully preserves the right of the supernatural, is in many ways like the modern view of historical reasoning as
completely objective.

7. Despite Oden's emphasis on the community, it is not clear
whether being genuinely postmodern is a matter of individual biog-
raphy, or whether one can be genuinely postmodern without having
ever adopted and lived out all of modernity's mentality, as he did.
What about the person who is thoroughly conversant with and has
studied deeply within modernity, but who has never really accepted
it? If such a person develops an orthodox theology, in light of mo-

dernity, but does not accept its claims, is such a person postmodern? Or must he or she first be converted to modernity before becoming postmodern?

We have not heard the last of Oden's proposal, only the beginning. It is an excitingly fresh wind blowing from an unexpected corner. We look forward to further profitable contributions.

4

Escape to Reason

Francis Schaeffer

It may seem strange to some readers that I should treat Francis Schaeffer in a consideration of postmodernism. Schaeffer did his major work in the 1960s and 1970s, before the word *postmodernism* was even invented, and before the demise of modernity had become evident. Surely it must be an anachronism to speak of his work as a response to postmodernity.

In one sense, of course, this charge is correct. For postmodernism as a movement had not really burst on the scene. Yet it is also true that periods do not simply fit within exact time designations, that they do not merely abut one another. Thomas Oden is right in his contention that in some ways what is identified as postmodernism should actually be considered ultramodernism, and is an outgrowth of certain tendencies at work within the modern period. There are always forerunners, vanguards, of any movement, and the phenomena of postmodernism appeared on the European Continent before they manifested themselves in North America. It was with these European intellectuals that Schaeffer worked. Although the tendencies and the views that he describes include a mixture of what we might today call modern and postmodern ideas, there is a sufficient amount of the latter to qualify his work as a response to postmodernism. What he was reacting to was postmodernism, but before anyone, including the adherents themselves, knew what it was. That this is genuinely the case can be seen from Schaeffer's assessment of the results of *musique concrète*: "There can be no other terminus when antithesis dies, when relativism is born and when the possibility of finding any universal which would make sense of the particulars is denied."[1] Here are the basics of postmodernism: the loss of logical antithesis, a thoroughgoing relativism, and the impossibility of any holoscopic metaphysical synthesis, or metanarrative. Thus, in many ways Schaeffer was ahead of his time. He was dealing with a movement, still in somewhat mixed form, that was to become more universally experienced.

Schaeffer founded and operated the L'Abri House, a retreat house to which intellectuals came for a time of study, reflection, and discussion, as well as working physically on the grounds. He also spoke widely on college campuses and in other settings with both students and intellectuals. When he became ill with cancer and went to the Mayo Clinic in Rochester, Minnesota, for treatment, he founded an American version of L'Abri near Rochester. Through his books, his thought also became more widely known.

Analysis of the Situation

Schaeffer believes that a movement began in the nineteenth century that has borne fruit in the twentieth century as late modernism. Prior to about 1890 in Europe and about 1935 in the United States, everyone was working with presuppositions which, epistemologically and methodologically, were basically the same and accorded well with Christian presuppositions. One of these was that there are absolutes, in both the areas of being and of morals. That meant that if something was true, its contradictory was false. Although people might disagree about what was true or right, at least they could communicate with one another, for they were talking about the same thing and agreed that the differences between them were objective differences, not merely subjective feelings. If something was true, then the opposite was false. In morality, if something was right, then the opposite was wrong. In other words, there was genuine antithesis. It was possible to communicate because people understood that if something was A, it was not simultaneously not-A. Whether your conversation partner agreed with you, he or she at least understood what you were saying. The non-Christian may not have had a sufficient basis for

---

1. Francis A. Schaeffer, *The God Who Is There* (Downers Grove, Ill.: InterVarsity, 1968), p. 38.

holding this view, but at least went on in romantic fashion, holding to these absolutes.[2] Thus, it was possible to engage in traditional apologetics with the unbeliever, because such a person would at least understand what the Christian was saying. Historic Christianity, Schaeffer would insist, rests on the basis of antithesis. Without that, it is meaningless.[3]

All of that has changed in the latter half of the twentieth century, however, according to Schaeffer. The dates mentioned earlier mark what Schaeffer calls the *line of despair*. Before that time, people were functioning on the basis of absolutes, even if they had only romantic grounds for holding these. After those dates, however, they slipped below the line of despair. This despair began in the discipline of philosophy, and spread successively to art, music, general culture, and, finally, theology. It did not come into a position of dominance overnight, but spread gradually and in three ways or directions. It spread geographically. First, beginning in Germany, it spread throughout Europe, then across the Channel to England, and then across the Atlantic Ocean to America. Second, it spread throughout society, beginning with the real intellectuals, then to the more educated, then to the workers, and finally to the upper middle class. Third, it spread from one discipline to another, as indicated above.[4]

It is essential, Schaeffer says, to understand this change and to present our Christian message in light of it. If we proceed as if nothing has changed and try to evangelize persons below the line of despair as if they were still above it, we will be ineffectual. We will simply beat the air.[5]

Schaeffer believes that the roots of this shift began with the German philosopher, Georg Hegel. Previously, Westerners thought in terms of antithesis. This, however, was related to the idea of cause and effect, in a horizontal, straight line. One event caused another, which then, in turn, caused yet another. For this cause–effect straight-line relationship, Hegel substituted the dialectic, with thesis, antithesis, and synthesis. Instead of a straight line, Hegel introduced a triangle. An event or movement arises, which is the thesis. Then its opposite—the antithesis—arises to oppose it. In the older, rational,

2. Ibid., pp. 13–14.
3. Ibid., p. 15.
4. Ibid., p. 16.
5. Ibid.

view, if one of these is true, then the other is necessarily false. In Hegel's understanding, however, these two are synthesized. Out of the opposition comes a new truth. Although the loss of the antithetical relationship of contradictories led to the line of despair, in Schaeffer's understanding, Hegel himself never slipped below it. Thinking that the antitheses could be resolved by reason, he remained an idealist and thus an optimist.[6]

Søren Kierkegaard followed Hegel, and to a large extent, his thought was a reaction to Hegel as well as to the Danish state church of the day. Kierkegaard did not believe it was possible to achieve by reason the synthesis of opposites about which Hegel wrote. Indeed, one of his books is entitled *Either-Or*. He says in one place, "Either-or is the road to heaven; both-and is the road to hell." If rational or logical synthesis could not be achieved, then it was not possible to have a faith based on logical reasoning. Instead, a leap of faith, in the absence of and even in contradiction to reason, must be made. This was a major step in the history of human thought. Schaeffer says, "But the important thing about him is that, when he put forth the concept of a leap of faith, he became in a real way the father of all modern existential thought, both secular and theological."[7] Kierkegaard had clearly slipped below the line of despair.

Prior to this time, living above the line of despair, philosophers had attempted to develop a worldview, an effort to interpret the whole of reality from within one's own experience. This was a matter of drawing a circle that would encompass everything within it. This was humanism, for it started from one's own human self. It also was rationalism, for it attempted to construct this circle using human reason. The history of philosophy was, then, a series of such circles being drawn by different philosophers, each of whom crossed out the circle drawn by the person immediately before him and replaced it with a "better" version. This was an optimistic belief that by their own reason, finite humans could find a unity within the diversity. The differences among them were in terms of where that circle should be drawn and what should be included within it.[8]

6. Ibid., pp. 20–21.
7. Ibid., p. 22.
8. Ibid., p. 17.

All this changed below the line of despair. Now Kierkegaard and those who followed him abandoned the idea of being able to draw a circle that would include everything. Now if rationalistic humanity wants to deal with the real things of life, such as purpose, significance, and the reality of love, it must be done by a nonrational leap of faith. This involves a major dichotomy:[9]

THE NONRATIONAL AND NONLOGICAL	Existential experience; the final experience; the first-order experience.
THE RATIONAL AND LOGICAL	Only particulars, no purpose, no meaning. Man is a machine.

Schaeffer acknowledges that at first glance this appears to apply only to the more existential philosophies, as contrasted with what he calls the "defining philosophy," by which he means the ordinary language philosophy or analytical philosophy. Yet he contends that there is a major point of agreement between the two, namely, that it is not possible to construct a comprehensive metaphysic that accounts for both parts of reality, the realm of rational knowledge and the realm of values. In this sense, both are antiphilosophies, for both are below the line of despair.[10]

A word of explanation is in order regarding Schaeffer's concept of despair. That word frequently arouses in us images of hopelessness, despondency, emotional anguish. This is not necessarily involved for those below the line of despair. They have given up the expectation of giving a rational basis to their hopes and values, but they may not yet have experienced the full significance and implications of this. They may continue to function very well with such a situation. Their hope may not have any real basis, but that does not mean that they do not have hope.

What has happened in philosophy has also spread to other intellectual disciplines and areas of culture. Schaeffer points out that sometimes bizarre means, such as the use of drugs or Eastern mysticism, are utilized to attempt to obtain the final experience or to try to make some sense of life, which cannot be obtained by the use of rational understanding.[11]

9. Ibid., p. 22.
10. Ibid.
11. Ibid., pp. 27–28.

In many ways, music, art, and literature are also means of expression of a view of life. So Schaeffer traces this development of the line of despair to art, and maintains that Van Gogh, Gauguin, Cézanne, Picasso, Mondrian, Dada, Marcel Duchamp, the Happenings, and the Environments all express this same sort of despair. In fact, the name of Dada illustrates this point. The name was selected by randomly placing a finger in a French dictionary and landing on the word *dada,* which means a child's rocking horse.[12]

In music, Schaeffer illustrates by use of *musique concréte*, in particular one composition, in which out of random chance sounds a voice arises, speaking Greek. Then gradually, the voice begins to degenerate and fall apart. This, Schaeffer feels, is an indication of the philosophy that fails to find any coherent explanation of the whole of reality.[13] In the general culture, he mentions especially Henry Miller, John Osborne, Dylan Thomas, modern cinema, the mass media, and the Beatles. Especially interesting is Schaeffer's interpretation of philosophic homosexuality. This illustrates the rejection of any sense of antithesis, by denying the distinction between male and female.[14]

In all these fields, despite the variety of expressions, Schaeffer would maintain that we are dealing with one common unifying factor: the rejection of any sense of antithesis, where a proposition and its contradictory cannot both be true. This is the point we as Christians must maintain. If we were to continue to hold to an orthodox theology but give up this important distinctive, we will have nothing left to say to the non-Christian.[15]

This trend, which began with philosophy and has worked through the various disciplines, came finally to theology. Here Schaeffer feels that Karl Barth, although he did not acknowledge his debt to Kierkegaard after the first edition of the *Epistle to the Romans*, was the doorway into the line of despair for theology. Here, as in the other realms of endeavor, there is a division of the rational and logical from the nonrational and nonlogical. In the former realm, one views Scripture as full of mistakes, and there is pessimism; in the latter, there is a crisis first-order experience, where

12. Ibid., pp. 30–36.
13. Ibid., pp. 37–38.
14. Ibid., p. 39.
15. Ibid., p. 47.

faith is an optimistic leap without verification or communicable content.[16]

The Human Predicament

This approach to reality has created an unusual predicament: humans living by this late-twentieth-century philosophy are caught in a tension. They cannot live with the implications of their position. This was true, for example, of existentialists Albert Camus and Jean-Paul Sartre. Sartre criticized Camus for inconsistency. In Schaeffer's view, this stems from his belief that all humans are created in the image of God, which includes rationality, and this is still present in all humans. Although the logic of their view ought to lead to the belief that humans are machines, their fallenness does not lead to "machineness," but to "fallen-manness."[17] Even though rationalistic humans have given up the concept of antithesis, they are not able to live on this basis. They cannot even communicate to themselves in their own thinking, without assuming the antithesis, so that the thought "I love her" or "the blossom is lovely" stands in contrast to the idea that he dislikes her or that the blossom is ugly.[18]

Schaeffer provides a number of illustrations of the inability of modern man to live on the basis of the theory that he holds. Although that theory calls for an understanding of humans as machines, it is impossible to escape the fact of one's own mannishness. Schaeffer tells of traveling on the Mediterranean with a young atheist, who thought he would have some entertainment with Schaeffer when he heard he was a clergyman. The young man understood the implications of his position, and Schaeffer noticed that he had a lovely young wife, with whom he was obviously very much in love. Just as their conversation was ending, Schaeffer asked the man, "When you take your wife in your arms at night, can you be sure she is there?" With a trapped look, the man shouted, "No, I am not always sure she is there," and went to his cabin.[19]

Another better-known example is John Cage, who composed music by tossing coins, so that the notes he selected were on the basis

16. Ibid., p. 53.
17. Ibid., p. 63.
18. Ibid., pp. 55–56.
19. Ibid., pp. 63–64.

of pure chance. Later he developed a device that would select notes by chance, a mechanical conductor that works on cams, the motion of which is unpredictable; the musicians simply followed the direction. This was his expression of a philosophy of reality in which there is no overall rational or logical explanation tying together the many particulars. Cage at one point in his life became quite interested in mushrooms. He realized that if he were to incorrectly identify a poisonous mushroom, and then cook and eat it, he could die. He said, "I became aware that if I approached mushrooms in the spirit of my chance operations, I would die shortly. So I decided that I would not approach them that way."[20] Schaeffer considers this decision an indication of the inability to live on the basis of one's theory. He comments, "In other words, here is a man who is trying to teach the world what the universe intrinsically is and what the real philosophy of life is, and yet he cannot even apply it to picking mushrooms. If he were to go out into the woods and begin picking mushrooms by chance, within a couple of days there would be no Cage!"[21]

The Positive Case for Christianity

It is at this point that Schaeffer begins his positive case for Christianity. He contends that Christianity has the answer to the three fundamental needs of the human being. Only in Christianity, he would argue, is there a way to resolve the tension within which humans live. It is orthodox Christianity, with its insistence on the traditional understanding of truth, that can supply such an answer, which the new theology cannot.[22]

The first of these needs is a basis for belief in human personality. Until man understands who he is, there is no relief from the internal tension. There are really only two options in this regard: a personal beginning to everything or an impersonal beginning. The biblical picture of God and creation is of a personal being who by his own free choice brings into existence other personal beings, humans. The personality of God is seen in the doctrine of the Trinity, according to which, even before the creation of human persons, there was interrelationship and love among the three persons of the Trin-

---

20. Ibid., pp. 73–74. From an interview in the *New Yorker*.
21. Ibid., p. 74.
22. Ibid., p. 87.

ity. This personal God then created humans in his own image, as personal.[23]

The alternative to this is the idea that human personality resulted from the impersonal by chance. Schaeffer introduces the idea of two valleys in the Alps, one dry and the other containing a lake. A lake begins to form in the dry valley, occasioning the question of its source. If, when the lake stops rising, it can be determined that it has the same elevation as the lake in the other valley, you might conclude that the first lake was the source of the water that created the second. If, however, the level of the surface of the second lake is found to be twenty feet higher than that of the first lake, you would know that it cannot have come from it. Its source must be found elsewhere. That, says Schaeffer, is what personality is like. If it has come from the impersonal, it has risen higher than its source, but that cannot be the case.[24]

No adequate explanation has ever really been given of how personality can have arisen from the impersonal. All such purported explanations are only illusions, the use of words that do not really explain. The claim that personality has so arisen is a mystical leap. As such, it cannot really be lived with. Indeed, if this view were correct, then human beings would be lower than the other beings in nature. Schaeffer uses an imaginary illustration of a fish that lives in a universe in which there are only solids and liquids, but no free gases. It can survive and function as it swims in this universe. But suppose that, through a chance occurrence of evolution, this fish were to develop lungs. Would it now be higher or lower? Schaeffer's answer is that it would be lower, because whereas formerly it could live in its environment, now it would drown, and a creature that can live is higher than one that cannot. Here, however, is the human, with all sorts of hopes and desires, for love, morality, rationality, beauty, and communication. But these cannot be fulfilled if there is not an adequate solution to human personality. Sir Julian Huxley has admitted as much by saying that, although he is an atheist, somehow man functions better if he believes that God is there. This is, however, to say that in the long run, man functions better by acting on the assumption that a lie is true. In fact, if the impersonal assumption is correct, then the human is lower than moss or

23. Ibid.
24. Ibid., pp. 87–88.

grass, because it can be fulfilled, whereas the human cannot. Like the story of the fish, the unfulfillable is lower than the fulfillable.[25] Schaeffer believes that the student revolts of the 1960s are evidence that humanity cannot accept the rationalistic or naturalistic explanation of humanity. He maintains that the professors had been teaching that a human being is really basically a machine, and the universities had been treating students as if that is what they were. Their rebellion against such depersonalization is an eloquent testimony that the human recognizes the inadequacy and inaccuracy of such a characterization.[26]

The second question or problem of humans to which Christianity supplies the answer is the need for knowledge. In particular, modern man lacks a unity for the whole of reality. Without a unified answer to the whole of life, despair results. What has happened is that modern man has engaged in rationalism, that is, the attempt to explain everything by working out from himself. In so doing, in ignoring the truth of the God who is there, he has lost rationality.[27] What is necessary, if rationality is to be regained, is for the human to surrender his autonomy in all areas of life, including the intellectual.[28]

There is a God, however, a personal God who exists and has revealed himself to humans. This is possible because he has created humans in his own image and likeness, as a result of which they are able to understand his truth. God has spoken, in true propositional form, and he has made known the truth, not only about himself but also about humanity, history, and the universe. Schaeffer insists that the revelation God has given be understood as involved with the space–time universe, rather than separated into some upper realm. While it may seem to some who hold the new theology that the inability to refute it because it does not impinge on the actual empirical facts is an advantage, Schaeffer insists that the very opposite is the case. If it is not susceptible either to verification or to falsification, it cannot really be discussed.[29] The historicity of the first eleven chapters of Genesis is essential to maintaining the idea of real

25. Ibid., pp. 88–89.
26. Francis A. Schaeffer, *Genesis in Space and Time* (Downers Grove, Ill.: InterVarsity, 1972), p. 17.
27. Francis Schaeffer, *Escape from Reason* (Downers Grove, Ill.: InterVarsity, 1968), p. 82.
28. Ibid., p. 83.
29. *God Who Is There*, pp. 93–94.

truth.[30] Only taking seriously the truth God has revealed about himself and the universe gives us a framework within which to interpret facts.

The third area in which Christianity gives the answer to human need is in terms of man and his dilemma. By this is meant the strange contradiction about the human, his ability either to rise to great heights, or to sink to great depths of cruelty and tragedy. Anyone with moral sensitivity must be able to see this great contradiction. There are two possible interpretations of this human predicament, one being that its cause is metaphysical, the other that it is moral. To say that the human contradiction stems from a metaphysical cause is to attribute human wickedness to finitude, with the resulting human inability to deal with the factors that confront him. But if this is the case, Schaeffer contends, then there is no moral answer to the problem of evil and cruelty. For such is simply part of the way man is.[31]

At this point in the argument, Schaeffer introduces an illustration whose point is not entirely clear because he does not explain it. It appears, however, that the point he is trying to make is that humanity cannot accept the idea of right and wrong as simply products of how things are and, therefore, morally neutral. He tells of a Hindu who objected to his presentation of Christianity. It was apparent to Schaeffer that the young man was unaware of the problems with his own view, so Schaeffer asked him if it was not the case on his view that cruelty and noncruelty are the same thing, and he acknowledged that this was true. At this point the Hindu noticed that the student in whose rooms this conversation was taking place was standing over him, holding over his head the steaming kettle of boiling water he was preparing for tea and asked him what he was doing. The student replied, "Cruelty and noncruelty are the same thing," whereupon the Hindu departed.[32] Similarly, the Marquis de Sade, who was one of the early modern chemical determinists, saw that if everything is determined, then there is no right or wrong. Whatever *is*, is right. You can say that certain acts are nonsocial or that certain things produce disintegration, rather than integration, but "you can-

---

30. Francis A. Schaeffer, *Genesis in Space and Time* (Downers Grove, Ill.: Inter-Varsity, 1972), pp. 9–10.
31. *God Who Is There*, p. 100.
32. Ibid., p. 101.

not say that anything is right or wrong. Man is dead. Morality is dead."[33]

The historic Christian answer to this dilemma is that God, as non-determined, created man as nondetermined, and that man used this freedom to choose to revolt against God. This concept is difficult for much modern thought, which believes that humanity's actions are determined, but it is the key to the human dilemma. It means that humans as we now find them are abnormal, rather than the way they came from the hand of God. They are now separated from their creator, who is the only true reference point, as well as from one another. Thus, cruelty exists, but the person who is cruel to another is being untrue to the original and intended human nature. There must have been a real, space–time fall. By that, Schaeffer means that the fall was a real event, before which Adam was unfallen and after which he was fallen. Had we been there, we could have observed that event occurring. Without the first three chapters of Genesis as actual history, one takes away a true Christian position and one cannot give Christianity's answers to the human dilemma.[34]

The Christian answer means that there are now true moral absolutes. There is not some law behind God. God is as far back as one can get. The absolutes rest on the moral character of God. Morality is that which conforms to the character of God; immorality is that which does not. Made by God in his own image, man is expected to conform to God's moral law, and is guilty before the lawgiver if he fails to do so. Thus there is real moral guilt, and there is a possibility that God is able to remove this guilt. The Bible says that God has provided this solution in the sending of his Son into the world to die as a propitiatory and substitutionary sacrifice.[35]

Four important facts flow from this biblical answer, according to Schaeffer:

1. The God who is there is a good God.
2. There is hope for a solution to the human dilemma.
3. There is a sufficient basis for morality, for right and wrong.
4. There is adequate reason for fighting wrong.[36]

33. *Church at the End of the Twentieth Century*, p. 14.
34. *God Who Is There*, p. 104.
35. Ibid., pp. 105–6.
36. Ibid., pp. 106–7.

This latter point needs some elaboration. If we live in a world of nonabsolutes, how do we determine what is right and what is wrong? The Christian answer enables us to know that there is a basis greater than simply the mood of the moment. It also means, however, that the Christian must be the real radical in society, fighting against evil. Otherwise, one may be merely maintaining the status quo.[37]

Another major question, however, must be asked: How do we know that Christianity is true? Schaeffer uses this illustration. Suppose that you had a book that had been torn so that all that was left was about an inch of printed material on each page. From this, it would not be possible to determine what the full story was, yet most people would not conclude that what was there had simply come together by chance. Then, however, suppose that you found in the attic the missing portions of these pages, and fitted them together with what you had. It would then be possible to read the story and make sense of it. Schaeffer makes two observations. First, the portions of the pages by themselves would not enable one to figure out the story. Second, the person's reason is what enables him or her to recognize that the found pages fit the remaining pages, but then on the level of the whole personality, that individual enjoys reading the story. This would particularly be the case if the restored book opened a relationship to someone important to the person who found the pages.[38]

Schaeffer's point is that the remaining pages represent the abnormal world and abnormal humanity as we now find it, and the portions of the pages that are discovered represent the Scriptures, which not only tell us about God but about humanity and the world. Humans are not able, from the former, to correctly figure out the full truth. When, however, Scripture is examined, one can see that it now gives an explanation of what was obvious before, but without an explanation, namely, that humanity is not just the result of chance factors. This is not simply a leap of faith, but a rational seeing that the two parts fit together. Schaeffer says: "With the propositional communication from the personal God before us, not only the things of the cosmos and history match up but everything on the upper and lower stories matches too: grace and nature; a moral absolute and

37. Ibid., p. 107.
38. Ibid., p. 108.

morals; the universal point of reference and the particulars; and the emotional and aesthetic realities of man as well."[39]

Schaeffer contends that religious proof, philosophical proof, and scientific proof all follow the same rules, or must meet the same criteria. There are two:

1. The theory must not be self-contradictory and must be able to give an answer to the problem under consideration.
2. It must be possible to live consistently with the theory.[40]

In addition to the positive argument, there is the negative, the consideration of the competing alternatives. Schaeffer believes that with respect to the understanding of the human, by the time the trivial answers are eliminated, there are four basic possible answers that do not involve a mystical leap of faith:

1. A personal human being has been produced by impersonal forces, plus time and chance. This answer, however, fails, Schaeffer says, because it goes against all experience.
2. The human is really not personal, but is a machine, is dead. This answer, however, does not satisfy the second criterion, for no one can really live on the basis of believing oneself to be a machine.
3. In the future we will find a reasonable answer. This, however, fails because of two reasons. The first is that it is an evasion, which could be given as an answer to virtually any problem. The second is that it simply is not possible to live with this sort of suspended judgment. One must continue making moral judgments, and they must have some basis.
4. The scientific theory of relativity may at some point in the future prove to be an adequate explanation. This cannot, however, be applied to humans in this way. In physics, there is still an absolute—the speed of light. Thus scientific theories are not in a state of constant flux, which would be the case when applied to humans. Contrasted with these alternatives, Christianity can be seen to be a noncontradictory

39. Ibid., p. 109.
40. Ibid.

view, which explains the phenomena and can be lived with, both in scholarly pursuits and in life.[41]

Approaching the Non-Christian

Schaeffer is not interested in merely presenting a logical view. He is ultimately an evangelist, concerned to bring non-Christians to belief. He believes that it is possible to have a genuine exchange of ideas with the non-Christian because every human has been made in the image of God and still retains something of that, in terms of what Schaeffer calls "mannishness." It is important to realize that no exact rules can be laid down for how to do this. It is also important to remember that this person is of great value, and our communication with him or her must be done in love. It is also essential to understand that the non-Christian is living in tension. The reason for this is that the mannishness cannot be lost, and so it is not possible to live out consistently a view that rejects the Christian explanation. Everyone has presuppositions, whether they realize it or not. If the non-Christian lived consistently, he or she would come out at the logical implications of the non-Christian presuppositions. No one is able to do that, however, for each person is still in touch with the reality of the world, both in terms of the external world in all its forms and his or her own essential mannishness. The dilemma is that the more closely one lives out one's presuppositions as a non-Christian, the further removed one is from the real world, and the more closely one lives in contact with the real world, the more inconsistent one is with one's presuppositions.[42]

From the standpoint of dialogue, this inconsistency is a good thing, for it is what makes communication possible. If a person were fully consistent with his or her non-Christian presuppositions, there really would be no common ground for communication, but the inability to live out those presuppositions consistently creates some basis for such conversation.[43]

But how do we proceed in such a conversation? It is here that Schaeffer's unique approach emerges. Some Christians would think that the way to proceed would be to try to move a person away from

41. Ibid., pp. 110–11.
42. Ibid., pp. 119–25.
43. Ibid., p. 126.

the logical conclusions of his or her presuppositions, back closer to the Christian presuppositions. Schaeffer's strategy is the exact opposite: to try to push a person toward a more consistent living out of his or her presuppositions. This is to push the person toward the point where he or she ought to be, if not stopped short. Each person has built a roof over his or her head, as it were, as shield from the blows of the real world, whether external or internal. The task of the Christian is, therefore, to help remove that shield, so that the person is exposed to the full force of those blows. The order of exposure to truth is different from what some might expect: *"The truth that we let in first is not a dogmatic statement of the truth of the Scriptures but the truth of the external world and the truth of what man himself is."*[44] In a sense, this is similar to what has been done in the past in preaching the fact of hell and lostness before one is told of salvation. This is not easy work, for there will be resistance to removing the roof and exposing someone to danger. Sometimes, the person will come face to face with the tension, but will be unwilling to accept the solution. When that happens, it appears that one has left the person in a worse situation than before, but this is not unlike the situation of people who were preached to about hell, but did not accept salvation. It is the risk that must be taken. Indeed, there is a risk that the person may even commit suicide, but this road of exposure to the truth must be traveled if there is to be genuine faith in the biblical sense.[45]

Evaluation

In this pioneering effort to give an evangelical response to postmodernism, there is much that is commendable, but also a number of points at which there are weaknesses.

Positive

1. Schaeffer has done us a great service by recognizing and flagging the postmodern phenomenon early. In part this was because he had the advantage of being located in Europe, where its manifestation surfaced considerably earlier than in the United States. He worked, of course, with the disadvantage of not having the categories that were later to become

44. Ibid., p. 129.
45. Ibid., pp. 129–31.

available as the explicit form of the postmodern movement became more detailed.

2. Schaeffer has correctly seen that the present ideology has roots that go back a considerable distance, at least to the nineteenth century, and has identified some of those early trends.

3. Schaeffer has seen the interconnection of fields, whereby cultural trends do not simply exist in isolation within one discipline, but spread to others, like waves radiating outward.

4. Schaeffer has correctly seen the major shift that has taken place and is taking place under the impact of postmodernism.

5. Schaeffer has seen the interconnection between Christian theology and the rest of culture. What occurs in other fields will inevitably also reach to theology.

6. Schaeffer has correctly seen that the Christian faith cannot be made to appear rational and desirable to a current postmodern person on his or her own terms. There is a necessity of pushing that person to live out the consequences of the view held, and to find that those cannot be lived with.

7. Schaeffer has seen that there is and must be a clear antithesis between the Christian faith and its theology, on the one hand, and the postmodern ideology on the other. He has, accordingly, refused to compromise the Christian faith by attempting to accommodate it to postmodernism.

Negative

1. There is some oversimplification of the analysis. Because Schaeffer is not a specialist in any of the areas he deals with, whether art, music, or literature, he selects those representatives whose work fits his theory. Specialists in those disciplines, however, find the overall hypothesis to be superficial, even misleading, in some cases.

2. Schaeffer does not take the analysis of the problem back far enough. He believes that the problem really began with Hegel's dialectic, in which opposing theses were synthesized. Yet he apparently does not realize that Hegel was attempting to respond to Kant's *Critique of Pure Reason*, according to which the attempt to apply the categories of the understanding to objects beyond sense experience leads to contra-

dictions or "antinomies." If one rejects Hegel's solution, then he is still confronted with Kant's problem.

3. Schaeffer seems to assume that Christianity is really the only viable alternative to the irrationalism he has been describing. On such an analysis, when pushed to the conclusion of one's conception, one must either choose Christianity or irrationalism. Is this the case, however? In today's pluralistic environment, it seems important to show how the other religious options fail to fulfill the human need for rationality.

4. There is a basically rationalist assumption here that overlooks the place that nonrational factors play in beliefs and behavior. The assumption is that if one sees the irrationality of a world that is not built on the basis of Christian theism, one will become a Christian. There are, however, other factors that stand in the way of people becoming followers of Jesus Christ. For if one does, Christ makes certain demands and has certain expectations of one, expectations the natural human in sin finds distasteful, to say the least. Too large a rearrangement of one's life is in order. This side of humans, which some psychoanalysts have seen very clearly, does not seem to enter into Schaeffer's analysis.

Part 3

Positive Responses to Postmodernism

5

To Boldly Go Where No Evangelical Has Gone Before

Stanley Grenz

One evangelical who has been quite vocal in calling for evangelicals
to formulate an apologetic and a theology in light of the phenomenon of postmodernism is Stanley Grenz of Carey Theological College in Vancouver, British Columbia. He urges evangelicals to take
seriously the challenge of postmodernism and to engage in a thorough "revisioning" of their theology in light of it. It will be the purpose of this chapter to examine and evaluate his proposal as a viable
response to postmodernism.

The Description of the Present Situation

Grenz's view of postmodernism is key to understanding and evalu-
ating his proposal. He indicates that postmodernism is not simply a
chronological period, but a broad cultural phenomenon. The term
came into use in the 1930s first as a designation of certain trends in
the arts and then as a label for a new type of architecture. By the
1970s, it had come to represent certain theories in university English
and philosophy departments and eventually to designate a broader,
more diffuse cultural phenomenon. His initial definition is in relationship to the modern era: "Whatever else it might be, as the name
suggests, postmodernism is the quest to move beyond modernism.
Specifically, it is a rejection of the modern mind-set, but under the

conditions of modernism. Therefore, to understand postmodern thinking we must view it in the context of the modern world which gave it birth and against which it is reacting."[1]

Description of the Modern Mind

To understand postmodernism as Grenz understands it, we must examine his depiction of modernism. Historically, the modern period can be dated from the beginning of the Enlightenment, which followed the Thirty Years' War. Grenz believes, however, that the stage was set for the Enlightenment, which placed humanity at the center of reality. Two individuals, the philosopher René Descartes and the scientist Isaac Newton, made the major contributions to this new orientation that soon gripped the world. Both men elevated human reason as the means of discovering the systematic truth present in the orderly world. Descartes was seeking for some certain and absolute truth, and he began his search by endeavoring to doubt absolutely everything. This he was able to do, but with one significant exception: he could not doubt that he was doubting. Since this was the case, he was certain of his own existence. From this beginning point, by a method of systematic deduction, Descartes developed his whole philosophy. Human nature, according to Descartes, is a thinking substance, and the human person is defined as an autonomous rational subject. Newton provided the scientific framework by picturing the physical world as a machine with laws and a regularity that could be discovered by the human mind. Grenz observes: "The modern human, therefore, is Descartes' autonomous, rational substance encountering Newton's mechanistic world."[2] The intellectual endeavor, then, is a matter of the rational individual examining the universe to unlock its secrets for the purpose of organizing life rationally and seeking to improve the quality of life through technology. This intellectual search for truth is based on three major epistemological Enlightenment assumptions:

1. Knowledge is certain. All of reality is to be scrutinized by reason, using a method that can demonstrate the essential correctness

1. Stanley J. Grenz, "Star Trek and the Next Generation: Postmodernity and the Future of Evangelical Theology," in *The Challenge of Postmodernism: An Evangelical Engagement*, ed. David S. Dockery (Wheaton, Ill.: Victor, 1995), p. 90.
2. Ibid., pp. 90–91.

of philosophic, scientific, religious, moral, and political doctrines. What is sought is universal truth in the form of correct statements.[3]

2. Knowledge is objective. The ideal intellectual is a dispassionate knower, who stands apart from being a conditioned observer, and from a vantage point outside the flux of history gains a sort of "God's-eye view" of the universe—if there were a God. As the scientific project is divided into separate and narrow disciplines, specialists, who are neutral observers who know more and more about less and less, emerge as the models and the heroes.[4]

3. Knowledge is inherently good. It is always better to know than not to know, and ignorance is a great evil. This being the case, no justification needed to be given for the scientific enterprise, since its results were unquestionably good. As a result, the Enlightenment was optimistic. Technology together with education will eventually enable us to master nature and overcome all the problems of the human race. Social bondage will also be overcome.[5]

This optimism, together with the emphasis on reason, led to a high value being placed on freedom, usually conceived of as individual freedom. Any claimed benefits that either curtail freedom or are seen to be based on some eternal authority, rather than reason and experience, must be rejected. The Enlightenment ideal is the "autonomous self, the self-determining subject who exists outside of tradition or community."[6]

Description of Postmodernity

This modern synthesis held primacy for several centuries. Until the 1970s, there was no full-scale frontal assault on it, but there had been isolated opposition, of which the first volley was fired by Nietzsche in the late nineteenth century, according to Grenz.[7]

The immediate impulse for the dismantling of the modern mind was a theory of literary criticism known as deconstruction, which arose as a response to structuralism. Structuralists contended that in the attempt to make sense out of the meaninglessness of life cultures develop literary texts. Literature provides categories for organizing

3. Ibid., p. 91.
4. Ibid.
5. Ibid.
6. Ibid., p. 92.
7. Ibid.

and understanding our experience of reality. Some structuralists also added that all societies and cultures have a common, unvarying structure that they then reflect in the stories they compose.[8]

Deconstructionists then rejected this structuralist theory, thus earning the title of "poststructuralists." Rather than the meaning being inherent in the text, placed there by the society that produced it, meaning emerges only as the interpreter enters into dialogue with the text. Consequently, there are as many meanings of the text as there are readers. For that matter, there are as many meanings as there are readings, as there may be more than one meaning for the same reader at different readings of the same text.[9]

Deconstructive philosophers took this approach to literary criticism and made it the basis for an all-encompassing theory of knowledge and reality of the world as a whole. Just as there is no inherent meaning in texts, which the reader attempts to discover and extract, so also reality as a whole does not contain an objective meaning. Reality can be read differently by different observers. The meaning of reality is dependent on the knower, and each knower has a somewhat different perspective he or she brings to the knowing experience. There is no one meaning of the world, no transcendent center to reality as a whole. In the final analysis, the world is only an arena of one person's interpretation against another's. Jacques Derridá, on the basis of ideas such as this, calls for the destruction both of "onto-theology" (the attempt to give ontological descriptions of reality) and "metaphysics of presence" (the belief that something transcendent is present within reality).[10]

Other deconstructionist philosophers elaborated and extended this theory. Michael Foucault, for example, contended that every interpretation is put forward by those in power and is thus an exercise of power. Naming something is doing violence to that which is named. Social institutions similarly do violence by imposing their own interpretations on the flux of experience. While Francis Bacon sought knowledge to gain power over nature, Foucault insists that every assertion of knowledge is an act of power.[11]

8. Ibid.
9. Ibid., p. 93.
10. *A Primer on Postmodernism* (Grand Rapids: Eerdmans, 1996), pp. 138–50.
11. "Star Trek," p. 93; *Primer on Postmodernism*, pp. 124–38.

Richard Rorty is the final philosopher whose views Grenz examines. Rorty jettisons the older view of truth as correspondence of the mind or language to the objects referred to, and measured by either comparing the words to the objects or finding the coherence of the statements with one another. Instead of attempting to find truth in the sense of correspondence to reality, we should be satisfied with interpretation. Although Grenz does not specifically mention it, Rorty's position is that words do not refer to any object outside language, but only to other words.[12] Instead of "systematic philosophy," which would presuppose a single unifying pattern to reality, he proposes "edifying philosophy," which seeks to continue a conversation rather than to discover truth.[13]

Unlike earlier generations, which looked for a unifying worldview that tied together the various elements of the universe, postmodernism does not believe any such unity exists. All is diversity and difference. Even the concept of a world contains the assumption of an objective unity or coherent whole to be found "out there." This postmodernism denies.

Postmodernism rejects each of the modern assumptions about the nature of knowledge. The inherent goodness of knowledge is rejected, for example. There is not an optimism, a confidence that progress is being made and must be made. This is seen in several areas. One is economic: generation X does not anticipate experiencing better economic circumstances than their parents experienced. Further, they do not expect that technology will solve the problems of the planet. There is ecological concern about the fragile condition of life and about the danger of an extensive war, so that both with respect to other peoples and to the rest of our planet, cooperation must replace the ideal of conquest.[14]

Postmodernism also rejects the idea that knowledge is completely rational and certain. Reason is not the sole means of gaining and judging knowledge. Since truth is nonrational, there are other means of discovering it, including emotions and intuition.[15]

12. *Primer on Postmodernism*, pp. 152–53.
13. "Star Trek," p. 93.
14. Ibid., p. 94.
15. Ibid., Grenz actually says "emotions and the institution," but this appears to be a misprint.

Finally, postmodernism rejects the idea that knowledge is objective. That view was based on the belief in an objective, rational order waiting to be discovered by the knower. That was a mechanistic model, with a dualistic epistemology. Rather, reality is now seen as relative, indeterminate, and discriminatory. Knowledge is personal and relational, historically and culturally conditioned, and therefore always incomplete.[16]

The model of the dispassionate, autonomous knower must therefore be abandoned. Since truth is not eternal and unitary, and since we are conditioned by our social and historical setting, all knowledge is also similarly limited and relative. Rather than being individual, truth is social or a product of the community of which the knower is a part. The specific truths we accept, as well as the very conception of truth that we hold are conditioned by the group to which we belong. This means that truth is relative to that community. The Enlightenment ideal of seeking for a single, universal, timeless, supracultural truth, true for everyone at all times and in all places, has been abandoned. Instead, truth is truth for a specific community. It is what fits within that community. It consists in the ground rules that facilitate the well-being of that community.[17]

Grenz believes that these contrasting approaches to truth can be seen in the two series of the "Star Trek" television program. The original series was representative of the modern mind.[18] "Star Trek: The Next Generation," on the other hand, presents the postmodern view of things.[19]

This, then, is postmodernism as Grenz sees it. The idea of a unified truth embedded in the universe and waiting to be discovered has been replaced by a universe that is historical, relational, and personal. The model of the dispassionate individual intellectual who discovers universal, unconditioned truth has been replaced by the idea that truth is historically and culturally conditioned and therefore relative to the group of which one is a part. Truth is social rather than individual. The method of arriving at the truth is not simply through rational investigation, but includes such affective factors as emotions and intuition. The optimistic hope of overcoming all soci-

16. Ibid., p. 94.
17. Ibid., pp. 94–95.
18. Ibid., p. 92.
19. Ibid., p. 95.

ety's problems by the use of technology has been replaced by a concern about the economic and ecological future of our country and our globe.

The Description of Evangelicalism

What, then, is Grenz's picture of evangelicalism? He contends that although it frequently claims to be a rejection of modernity, evangelicalism is actually based on the Enlightenment. The evangelical movement was born in the early modern period and in North America reached its high point at the height of the modern period. Grenz goes even further than this, however, and says that evangelicals *are* Enlightenment thinkers. This is seen in the way in which evangelicals react to modernity. They have always used the tools of modernity, borrowing heavily from the scientific method.[20] When evangelicals attempted to respond to the secularism of late modernity, these tendencies became especially evident. Much of their effort was devoted to an apologetic that would demonstrate the credibility of the Christian faith to a culture that exalts reason and science.[21]

Evangelicalism also is generally concerned about the propositional content of the faith. Thus, its systematic theologies generally aim to provide a logical presentation of truth, a "summary or synopsis of the themes of teaching in Holy Scripture."[22] This is because traditional evangelicalism has defined itself in terms of a set of doctrines believed.[23]

All of this means, according to Grenz, that evangelicals have done well in developing a vision of the Christian faith for the old "Star Trek Society." This, however, will no longer do, for our society is moving beyond that period and that orientation. A new paradigm for evangelicalism must be developed to fit this new and different situation. Western culture, all the way from pop culture to academia, is moving into postmodernity. The younger generation, who take for granted the information age, MTV, and channel surfing, are even more committed to the postmodern vision of reality. This generation is not so impressed as their predecessors with linear thinking, ratio-

20. Ibid., p. 96; *Revisioning Evangelical Theology: A Fresh Agenda for the 21st Century* (Downers Grove, Ill.: InterVarsity, 1993), pp. 65–66.
21. *Primer on Postmodernism*, pp. 161–62.
22. *Revisioning Evangelical Theology*, p. 62.
23. Ibid., p. 26.

nal argumentation, and final answers. This is a clarion call to evangelicals to understand what is happening and to respond in the most appropriate way.[24]

Assessment of Postmodernism

Grenz urges a careful assessment of postmodernity. Is it something we can adopt and find useful, or should we be careful and skeptical about its desirability and utility? He devotes considerable attention to this large question.

He first notes that as evangelicals we cannot go all the way with postmodernism's tenets. In particular, we cannot accept its skepticism. It most certainly eliminates objective truth, the idea that truth is a matter of human statements. In particular, Grenz believes that most traditional thinkers define truth as correspondence of propositions to reality "out there." The postmodern understanding has some far-reaching implications: "This rejection of the correspondence theory not only leads to a skepticism that undercuts the idea of objective truth in general; it also undermines the Christian claims that our doctrinal formulations state objective truth."[25] The clash with Christian sympathies lies deeper than merely the loss of the correspondence theory of truth, however, in Grenz's view. "More radical . . . is the postmodern despair of the quest to discover all-encompassing truth."[26] That arises from postmodernism's idea that reality is not a unified whole with a transcendent center. Grenz is clear and emphatic in his rejection of such a stance.[27]

Grenz's response to this loss of unity of reality is in terms of the postmodern focus on "story." Christians believe that there is one unifying story, a single history, including all peoples and all times. This story is the biblical narrative of God acting to save fallen humankind, and above all, the incarnation of Christ. While agreeing with postmodernism that all human interpretations are in some sense and to some degree deficient, Grenz maintains that interpretations are not all *equally* invalid. The conflicting interpretations can be evaluated according to a single criterion. Because we believe that in Jesus Christ the Word became flesh, the story of God's action in

---

24. *Primer on Postmodernism*, p. 163.
25. Ibid.
26. Ibid.
27. Ibid., pp. 163–64.

Jesus Christ is the criterion by which all interpretations of reality are to be measured.[28]

This biblical narrative brings all of humankind into a single history. Consequently, this story embodies *the* truth, of and for all humankind. The gospel is not only *for us.* It is good news *for all.* It fulfills the longings and aspirations of all peoples, and therefore, whether we acknowledge it or not, it is our *human* narrative. Thus, we cannot buy into the loss of the "metanarrative," as Lyotard has put it.[29]

Having issued this disclaimer, however, Grenz proceeds to indicate his common ground with postmodernism in its rejection of the fundamental Enlightenment assumptions. One of these is the Enlightenment assumption that "knowledge is objective and hence dispassionate." Together with postmodernism, Grenz denies that reason, operating through the scientific method, is the only measure of truth. Rather, with the pietists, he affirms that certain aspects of truth lie outside reason.[30]

Grenz takes his criticism of reason a step further. We must always take a cautious, even distrustful stance toward human reason. As Christian theology reminds us, humanity is fallen, and this means that sin sometimes blinds the human mind. Grenz sees a parallel between postmodernism's contention that all our intellectual endeavors are conditioned by our own participation and the Christian understanding of the human predicament. Although postmodernity was dealing with epistemology rather than spirituality, we can also see the point there. It is not possible to stand outside the historical process and gain universal, unconditioned truth. Just as these personal convictions and commitments color our search for knowledge, so with Augustine, Grenz feels that they facilitate the search for understanding.[31]

Recent history contributes to our acceptance of the postmodern criticism of the inherent goodness of knowledge. Although knowledge has brought many benefits, the knowledge explosion cannot produce a humanly constructed utopia. Technological advances can be applied either for good or for evil. Based on our experience with

28. Ibid., pp. 164–65.
29. Ibid.
30. Ibid., p. 166.
31. Ibid., pp. 166–67.

the splitting of the atom, for example, Grenz wonders whether our ability to alter the world, resulting from the application of the scientific method, outstrips our moral resolve.[32]

The Christian understanding of the human situation provides a foundation for a critique of the Enlightenment view of human reason and knowledge. According to Christianity, the problem is not merely ignorance but a misdirected will. Thus, the removal of ignorance is insufficient apart from the renewal and redirection of the heart.[33]

These dimensions of the postmodern reaction to the Enlightenment suggest that postmodernism may have more to offer Christian theologians than one might have thought after Grenz's initial appraisal.[34]

Contours of a Postmodern Theology

The church, in Grenz's estimation, has a mandate to listen to the voices within the academy and the culture to understand the culture in which it finds itself and to live out the gospel within that culture. The description he has given us of postmodernism is intended to help meet the first part of that mandate. Now, however, he maintains that we must go beyond that and formulate a genuinely postmodern theology, taking these insights into account.[35]

By this agenda, however, Grenz does not mean merely a theology that responds to postmodernism's questions or perhaps attempts to rebut the contentions of postmodernism. If it were the former, it would simply be something of an evangelical version of Paul Tillich's "answering theology" or Grenz's "method of correlation." Rather, he is calling for a thorough revisioning of evangelical theology, beginning with a shift in the basis of definition of evangelicalism from primarily a theological system to a type of spirituality, focused on the experience of new birth.[36] Second, the locus of theology is revisioned. Rather than a summarization of the doctrinal teachings of the Bible, it is reflection on the beliefs of the community.[37] There is also to be a revisioning of the sources of theology.[38] For Grenz's

---

32. Ibid., p. 166.
33. Ibid., pp. 166–67.
34. Ibid.
35. "Star Trek," pp. 79–98.
36. *Revisioning Evangelical Theology*, p. 35.
37. Ibid., pp. 62, 64, 81, 85
38. Ibid., p. 88.

theological methodology calls for the employment of three sources: the Bible, the tradition of the church, and the culture. The latter is to supply the thought-forms for the expression of the message. Grenz says, "The social community in which the people of God participate contains its own cognitive tools—language, symbols, myths, and outlooks toward the world—that facilitate identity formation and the experience of reality."[39]

Finally, the nature of biblical authority is to be revisioned. Traditionally evangelicalism has moved from the idea of revelation to the doctrine that the Bible is an inspired preservation of that revelation and is therefore authoritative. But, says Grenz, "the assertion of the inspiration of Scripture cannot function as the theological premise from which bibliology emerges, nor as the focal point of our understanding of the relation between the Spirit and Scripture."[40] After examining two recent approaches to biblical authority, the canonical and the functional, he expresses agreement with them that throughout its history the church has confessed its belief in the inspiration of the biblical documents "because believers in every age hear in them the voice of the Spirit as they seek to struggle with the issues they face in their unique and ever-changing contexts."[41] Consequently, in Grenz's systematics, the doctrine of Scripture is not introduced as it traditionally is, early in the treatment. Rather, it does not enter until the second half of the book, under the doctrine of the Holy Spirit.[42]

Thus far, evangelicals have left the task of constructing a postmodern theology to the mainline theologians, who have come up with varied schemes. Grenz wants to propose at least the contours of an alternative to these in a genuinely postmodern evangelical theology.[43]

Postindividualistic

A postmodern evangelical theology must be postindividualistic. This is in keeping with postmodernism's rejection of the autonomous individual intellectual, who was the model of modernism's scholarship. We must not, of course, overlook the valid biblical em-

39. *Theology for the Community of God* (Nashville: Broadman & Holman, 1994), pp. 25–26.
40. *Revisioning Evangelical Theology*, p. 118.
41. Ibid., p. 120.
42. *Theology for the Community of God*, pp. 494–527.
43. *Primer on Postmodernism*, p. 167.

phasis on the individual, with God's concern for each individual, the responsibility of each individual before God, and the responsibility of the church to share the good news of the gospel with each individual person. Experientially, we have also seen enough totalitarianism so that we must guard against any tyranny of the whole over the individual, in whatever form. Yet, having said this, Grenz is also concerned about the invasion of the church by the ideas of radical individualism, such as the presentation of the gospel being made in such a way that it appears that God has saved us in isolation.[44]

What Grenz is urging us to avoid, however, is the idea that knowledge of any kind, including knowledge of God, is objective. The model of the knower, in any subject-matter field is not the neutral, knowing self, the individual ivory-tower specialist who explores his or her subject matter seeking to find a universal and complete body of timeless propositions about an objective given. In place of this self-determining individual who exists outside any tradition or community, postmodern evangelicalism will set the individual-within-community.[45]

Why, however, is this emphasis on community so crucial? Grenz offers two reasons. The first is that a "community of reference" is integral to the process of knowing. He says: "Individuals come to knowledge only by way of a cognitive framework mediated by the community in which they participate."[46] It appears that the community plays a role in supplying the cognitive framework necessary for knowledge, almost as the pure forms of space and time and the categories of the understanding did in Kant's analysis of pure reason.

A second reason is that the community of reference is crucial to identity formation. Our personal sense of identity emerges through telling our personal narratives, and this is always embedded in the story of the communities in which we participate. As Grenz puts it, "The community mediates to its members a transcendent story that includes traditions of virtue, common good and ultimate meaning."[47]

There are definite theological reasons why this communitarian approach must be incorporated into a postmodern theology. The Bible shows the importance of community—the community of God in the

44. Ibid., pp. 167–68.
45. Ibid., p. 168.
46. Ibid.
47. Ibid.

lives of believers. God's goal for them is the establishment of community in the highest sense. While we are saved as individuals, we are saved together and to be together. This is in turn based on a further doctrinal ground. God is a social Trinity and has created us in his image. His goal is that we might be the image of God, which involves not merely individual existence, but that of humans-in-relationship, thus reflecting the Trinity.[48]

Postrationalistic

Modernity made some significant gains through its emphasis on reason, for it freed society from a host of superstitions that plagued premodern peoples. Postmodern theology dare not give up this great Enlightenment gain to become anti-intellectual. Yet the postmodern critique of modernity reminds us that we are more than simply rational. And there are dimensions of reality the rational scientific method does not touch. Theology must retain a place for the concept of "mystery," not as an element of the irrational, alongside the rational, but as a reminder that God and everything in the world go beyond human rationality.[49]

Grenz offers at least three explications of this element of mystery. One is the nature of God. Rationalism, with its infatuation with the scientific method, makes God the object of human scrutiny. Theology becomes the cool, calculating dissecting of God, listing his attributes in the form of timeless propositions.[50]

A second reason is the nature of truth. Traditional theology, based on modernism, made truth a matter of correct propositions, corresponding to what they describe. While not wanting to abandon rational discourse, Grenz insists that we cannot remain fixated on the propositionalist approach, which believes that Christian truth is simply doctrinal formulations.[51]

The third reason for this needed shift is the nature of beliefs. As a postmodernist, Grenz holds that both knowledge and belief are socially and linguistically constituted. No experience occurs in a vacuum. Rather, experience and interpretive concepts are reciprocally related. On the one hand, our concepts facilitate the experiences we

48. Ibid., pp. 168–69.
49. Ibid., p. 17.
50. Ibid.
51. Ibid.

have. On the other hand, our experiences cause us to reflect on, even modify, the interpretive concepts we use to speak about our lives.[52]

When this understanding is applied to theology, important implications emerge. The very core of being a Christian is a personal encounter with Christ, which then shapes and molds us. Based on this encounter, we attempt to bring the diverse strands of our personal lives into an understandable whole through the use of certain categories, such as "sin" and "grace," "lost" and "saved," and others. This is the role of doctrinal propositions, to make sense out of life by recounting the story of a transformative religious experience. The reciprocal nature of propositions and experience, however, means that not only are propositions used to express the experience, but they also facilitate those experiences. They form the grid by means of which the believer now views all of life. They are second-order in nature, however: "They both serve the conversion experience and arise out of our new status as believers."[53]

Postdualistic

Modern thought was built on a fundamentally dualistic understanding of reality as mind and matter, and of human nature as soul and body. The latter distinction was especially prominent in the thought of Descartes. This dualism has made its way into Christian thought, with a strong emphasis on "saving souls" but with little concern for bodies, because we believe that the physical dimension of the person is of no eternal significance.[54]

Postmodern thought, however, increasingly sees humans as a unified whole. In this, Grenz believes, it is closer to ancient biblical anthropology than is the thought of many modern Christians. A postmodern theology must therefore be postdualistic. By this he means more than just putting together the soul and body the Enlightenment tore asunder. Rather, there must be an integration of the many dimensions of the human person into a single whole, including a new concern for the place of emotion and intuition in our lives. Grenz does not mean simply giving greater place to these affective dimensions of life alongside the rational, but "integrating the emotional-affective, as well as the bodily-sensual, with the intellectual-rational

52. Ibid.
53. Ibid., p. 171.
54. Ibid.

within the one human person. In other words, to borrow from "Star Trek: The Next Generation," we must be willing to acknowledge the dependency of the Counsellor Troi alongside the Spock (or Data) in each of us."[55]

Postnoeticentric

Grenz acknowledges that knowledge is *a* good. Consequently, there is no substitute for theological reflection. It is not, however, good as an end in itself. It is good only when it contributes to a good result, which, in the case of theology, is the building up of the person in spirituality. A postmodern theology, therefore, will never be satisfied with lists of propositions. Like the pietists, Grenz believes that there must be a "right heart," or the "right head" is dead. Beliefs are important because they shape conduct. Theology seeks to clarify our foundational belief structure.[56]

Evaluation

Having now examined at some length Grenz's treatment of postmodernism, the time has come to engage in some evaluative observations. There are both commendable features and issues.

Positive

1. Grenz has chosen to deal with a movement of great current importance. He thus displays real relevance in choosing to dialogue, not with philosophies that have passed their peak, but with one that, to all indications, will continue to grow in both strength and influence.
2. Grenz has shown the courage to be innovative, rather than merely to enunciate evangelical theology in the same familiar fashion. He seeks to be genuinely contemporary.
3. Grenz has correctly noted the Enlightenment ideal still sometimes found in the thought of evangelical theologians. As an example, the hermeneutical work of some evangelicals whole-heartedly adopts the method and presuppositions of E. D. Hirsch, allowing virtually no role for the Holy Spirit in interpretation. Grenz's ascription of a positive role

---

55. Ibid.
56. Ibid., p. 173.

for the Holy Spirit in the hermeneutical process is more in keeping with the Reformation heritage on this matter.

4. Grenz has correctly recognized that all knowledge is obtained by a knower who stands within a particular historical and cultural setting, and consequently, there is a degree of the relative within each scheme of conclusions. Some evangelical theologians do not feel the force of this concern.

5. Grenz takes seriously the corruption of the reason, which is part of total depravity. He therefore sees certain limitations on the power of the knower, particularly the secular thinker, to know and understand spiritual truth.

6. Grenz has correctly pointed out the danger of excessive individualism in evangelicalism. When one combines the influence of Western individualism with the natural inclination toward independence of many in the free church tradition, the priesthood of all believers becomes transmuted into the priesthood of *each* believer, which is a somewhat different matter. The latter often turns out to be something like "every one is entitled to his own opinion," which is quite different from what the Reformers had in mind with the doctrine of the priesthood of all believers.

Negative

There are a number of problems here, and of a variety of types. It is not primarily our purpose to evaluate Grenz's thought in terms of whether it is genuinely evangelical. Criticisms of this type have appeared and are appearing.[57] Criticism of his thought can be grouped into several clusters.

1. The first are problems connected with Grenz's depiction of postmodernism. There is some oversimplification in his description of postmodernism. A variety of influences contributing to current postmodernism, such as the new historicism, empirical theology,

---

57. Cf. R. Albert Mohler Jr., "The Integrity of the Evangelical Tradition and the Challenge of the Postmodern Paradigm," in *The Challenge of Postmodernism: An Evangelical Engagement,* ed. David S. Dockery (Wheaton, Ill.: Victor, 1995), pp. 78–81; Norman Gulley, *Systematic Theology,* vol. 1, *Prolegomena* (forthcoming), manuscript pp. 269–73; Glenn Monroe Galloway, "The Efficacy of Propositionalism: The Challenge of Philosophical Linguistics and Literary Theory to Evangelical Theology" (Ph.D. diss., Southern Baptist Theological Seminary, 1966), pp. 207–11; D. A. Carson, *The Gagging of God* (Grand Rapids: Zondervan, 1996), p. 481.

and neopragmatism, make the movement more complex than Grenz has pictured. The connections of postmodernism with certain trends within modernism cause some, such as Thomas Oden, to call it "ultramodernism." Some, such as Schleiermacher and Kierkegaard, who long ago protested the extremes of Enlightenment rationalism, should be taken into account. Nor does Grenz point out the beginnings of decline, dissent, and even defection taking place in deconstructive postmodernism.

2. A second set of issues relates to the accuracy of Grenz's depiction of evangelicalism. He seems essentially to argue that evangelicalism in the twentieth century, at least in its resurgence during and since the Second World War, is based on the Enlightenment approach and adopts the views of the modern mentality, but what he describes sounds more like the Protestant Scholasticism of the seventeenth and eighteenth centuries than it does like twentieth-century evangelicalism. One who perhaps most fully represents the type of theology that Grenz is discussing is Carl F. H. Henry. Yet it is notable that Henry has on several occasions and at considerable length criticized the same Enlightenment philosophy that Grenz rejects as a postmodern evangelical.[58] Other examples could also be given, such as Edward Carnell's appeal to the "third method" of knowing.[59] By identifying twentieth-century evangelicalism with the Enlightenment mentality, Grenz believes that by criticizing the modern mind and its Enlightenment presuppositions he has successful criticized traditional evangelicalism, but that belief may be more rhetorical than logical. It appears that the picture of evangelicalism has been something of a caricature.

Perhaps this could be exhibited more clearly by the use of a diagram.

A	B	C	D
Deconstructive	Stanley Grenz	Carl Henry	Enlightenment
Postmodernism	Revisioned	Traditional	Modern mind
	Evangelicalism	Evangelicalism	

58. E.g., *Remaking the Modern Mind, The Drift of Western Thought, God of the Ages or Gods of This Age,* and his magnum opus, *God and Revelation.*

59. Edward John Carnell, *Christian Commitment: An Apologetic* (New York: Macmillan, 1957), pp. 21–23, 32–116.

It appears that what Grenz has done is criticize D, drawing on the arguments and the culture of A. By identifying C (which also rejects some features of D) with D, he feels that he has successfully criticized C. While drawing on the arguments of A, he refuses to go all the way with A.

3. The third part of our critique relates to Grenz's own adoption of postmodernism. He is quite clear that evangelical theology must take on some of the characteristics of postmodernism, if it is to minister effectively in this postmodern age. His proposals for the type of theology it is to be embody that idea. Essentially he seems to be implying that by its nature evangelicalism is well suited to be a postmodern movement, but that in its twentieth-century form, rooted in the fundamentalist struggle with liberalism, it essentially took on the characteristics of the Enlightenment mind.

Yet Grenz insists that at a number of points evangelical theology must "stand its ground" over against postmodernism. It must not give up objectivity of truth to become irrational or anti-intellectual. It must not lose its emphasis on individual conversion and a personal relationship to Jesus Christ. It must resist the loss of any all-encompassing truth. While recognizing that all views are historically conditioned, it does not believe that all are equally valid. On the basis of their commitment to Jesus Christ and to the narrative based on God's action in him, evangelicals simply must reject the skepticism in much postmodernism.

The question, however, is on what grounds we are able to do that. If we accept the basic theses and presuppositions of postmodernism, can we stop short of its conclusions simply by saying, "For Christians, this is simply untenable" or something similar?[60] Can we use the arguments of those at position A, but stop short of that position by a simple act of refusal? Do we not have to engage in some sort of critique of the position more extensive than asserting that it conflicts with our Christian commitment? This seems, on the surface, to constitute some species of voluntarism, whereby one chooses not to accept a particular tenet of a view to which one is otherwise committed.

By the same token, if Grenz's assertions are to be taken as beliefs not only for him, but as objectively the way other evangelicals should do theology as well, there must be a more adequate reason

60. "Evangelical Theology II," p. 4.

for going partway with postmodernism, but not all the way, other than, "This is unacceptable to us." Why is it unacceptable? On what grounds should we reject it?

The criticism takes another form. Grenz contends that knowledge is relative to the group or community of which one is a part. That undoubtedly is the basis for rejecting the more radical conclusions of postmodernism. The question, however, is, Why this community rather than another, a non-Christian community? And within the broadly Christian realm, which of the countless subcommunities is the one within which our beliefs are to find their validity? Rather different doctrinal formulations are made by liberal Episcopalians and Southern Baptist fundamentalists, for example. Why one community rather than another? Without some answer to such questions, postmodern evangelicalism will sound like Emil Brunner's response to the question about how a Muslim hears "his master's voice" within the Koran, as a Christian does within the Bible: "We are not Muslims."[61]

There are some points at which it is questionable how genuinely postmodern Grenz's approach is. One of the major emphases of the new mood is globalization and multiculturalism. Yet Grenz's major work of theology is amazingly Eurocentric, containing profuse references to classical and twentieth-century Western theologians, but extremely few citations from feminist or third world theologians.[62]

4. Our final concern is how genuinely evangelical Grenz's approach can be considered. This is certainly a somewhat different conception of evangelicalism than has usually been thought of. In fact, in some ways, such as its emphases on narrative and the community, it seems to draw rather heavily on the postliberalism of someone like George Lindbeck.[63] There is an apparent tension in Grenz's thought, in which having rejected the usual evangelical doctrine in a particular area, he then says, in effect, "But of course, I also hold to . . . (the doctrine under discussion)." It is therefore often difficult to determine precisely what he does hold on a given doctrinal issue. Perhaps the ambiguity or ambivalence will be resolved more clearly in the future. In the meantime, however, some evangelical

61. H. Emil Brunner, *Our Faith* (New York: Scribner's, n.d.), p. 11.
62. See *Theology for the Community of God*, index.
63. Roger E. Olson asserts that Grenz explicitly agrees with Lindbeck's definition of doctrine ("Whales and Elephants: Both God's Creatures But Can They Meet?" *Pro Ecclesia* 4.2 [Spring 1995]: 180.

commentators have expressed doubt as to the legitimacy of terming Grenz's theology evangelical. None is stronger in raising this question than Donald Carson, who says, "With the best will in the world, I cannot see how Grenz's approach to Scripture can be called 'evangelical' in any useful sense."[64] But to the degree that in the desire to make his theology harmonious with postmodernism, it has modified received evangelicalism, it cannot serve as a valid option for us.

64. Carson, *The Gagging of God*, p. 481.

6

Theology Is Stranger Than It Used to Be

J. Richard Middleton and Brian J. Walsh

J. Richard Middleton and Brian J. Walsh several years ago co-authored a book in which they described and assessed Christianity as a worldview in relation to four essential questions:

1. our place or world (where are we?)
2. our self or identity (who are we?)
3. our understanding of good and evil (what's wrong?)
4. the solution to the problem (what's the remedy?)[1]

In light of the changing world, they proposed to revise that book. Their publisher, however, wisely, in their judgment, suggested a completely new book.[2] The execution of that project is the volume we are considering here. It attempts to describe and assess the changes that have taken place in the world with the decline and dis-integration of the modern orientation and the rise of postmodern-ism. The second half of the book seeks to employ the same four questions in showing how the biblical worldview bears on the postmodern condition. Whereas they had described the Christian worldview in *The Transforming Vision*, they now seek to nuance it in light of the new situation.

1. J. Richard Middleton and Brian J. Walsh, *The Transforming Vision: Shaping a Christian World View* (Downers Grove, Ill.: InterVarsity, 1984).
2. J. Richard Middleton and Brian J. Walsh, *Truth Is Stranger Than It Used to Be: Biblical Faith in a Postmodern Age* (Downers Grove, Ill.: InterVarsity, 1995), p. 4.

The title of their book, *Truth Is Stranger Than It Used to Be,* has a twofold reference. On the one hand, it refers to the shift in the understanding of truth from the modern ideal of perfect objectivity and correspondence to the facts, to the postmodern insistence on the relativity and conditioned nature of truth. On the other hand, however, it refers to a different approach to the Christian understanding of truth. A rereading of the Bible in light of the concerns raised by postmodernity leads to a modified conception. Whereas the conventional way of viewing the Bible in a modern framework was to look for timeless, propositional truths, the postmodern situation has led them to consider it primarily narrative in character. Thus, the postmodern situation, although a time of "crisis and tragedy," has actually led them to exciting dimensions of the Bible that they had formerly overlooked.[3]

Description of the Postmodern Situation

Any understanding of the postmodern situation requires understanding the modern situation, if for no other reason than the postmodern represents a reaction against and even a rejection of it. Middleton and Walsh believe that the defining statement could best be taken from John Dewey. He states four major characteristics of modernity:

1. A preoccupation with the natural, the this-worldly, rather than the otherworldly. It is thus a thoroughly secular view.
2. A rejection of any call for submission to ecclesiastical authority. There is instead an emphasis on the power of individual minds to attain the truths needed for life.
3. A belief in progress. The golden age lies *before* us, not behind us. We may attain it by application of human abilities.
4. The scientific method, producing inventions that control and harness nature to society's uses, is the method by which progress is to be made.[4]

Modernism has not attained its ideals, however. Believing that it could progressively build a better society, it has faltered and then fallen in the twentieth century. Actually, the entire foundation of the

3. Ibid., pp. 4–5.
4. Ibid., p. 14.

104

building was faulty, as is now apparent, and cannot be shored up. The atrocities of two World Wars, plus a great economic depression, have revealed the inadequacy of this view. The existentialists' criticisms were followed by a new surge of confidence in the 1950s, but it is apparent that the old problems have not been overcome. Middleton and Walsh comment:

> As we approach the end of the twentieth century, modernity is in radical decline. Its legitimating myths are no longer believed with any conviction. The old 'sacred canopy' of modern progress which had previously sheltered the inhabitants of modernity has blown off the fourth floor and the biting chill of anomie now settles on the 'naked public square.' The result is that we are exposed to radical insecurity and to what anthropologist Clifford Geertz calls the 'gravest sort of anxiety.'[5]

It is for reasons such as this that postmodernity has risen to prominence. Middleton and Walsh accordingly describe and analyze this movement in relationship to the four crucial questions they had posed earlier.

The View of Reality

Modernity had held to the objectivity and knowability of reality. By carefully guarding the objectivity of one's methodology, one could attain to truth, which was understood in terms of a correspondence view, namely, that our ideas correctly describe reality, which exists independently of any knower. The postmodern answer to the question, "where are we?" however, is: "we are in a reality we have constructed."[6] Reality, according to postmodernism, is a social construct. Using the old joke about the three umpires' discussion of balls and strikes, which they attribute to Walter Truett Anderson, they contrast three views of reality. The first umpire ("There's balls and there's strikes, and I call 'em the way they are") is the naive realist, assuming that his or her judgments correctly reflect the reality that they claim to describe. The second umpire ("There's balls and there's strikes, and I call 'em as I see 'em") is a perspectival realist (or perhaps a critical realist). The third umpire ("There's balls and

5. Ibid., p. 25.
6. Ibid., pp. 30–31.

there's strikes, and they ain't *nothin'* until I call 'em") is a radical perspectivalist. Many postmodern thinkers, according to Middleton and Walsh, are represented by this third umpire. They doubt whether there is anything "real" beyond our judgments. While pointing out that there is a significant difference between the second and third positions, Middleton and Walsh assert that "it is fair to say that the current predominance of these positions (both in the academy and on the street) represents the demise of the naive realism of modernity."[7]

Modernism, whether scholarly or popular, assumed that truth was arrived at by establishing a correspondence between an objectively "given" reality and the knower's thoughts or assertions. Postmodernism, however, considers such correspondence impossible, because we simply do not have access to "reality" apart from the concepts and language by which we represent that reality. We can never get outside our knowledge to know reality in some direct fashion. It is always mediated to us by our linguistic and conceptual constructions.[8]

Another way of putting this is that we always know reality as mediated through our worldview. In their earlier work, Middleton and Walsh had argued that everyone has a worldview. Thus, our knowledge of the world around us is structured by the worldview through which we experience it.[9]

Some postmodernists go further than this, however. While not necessarily denying that there is a world independent of our knowledge, they do deny that the world has any objective features that could serve as norms or criteria for truth and goodness, to which we might appeal. Any such norms are always social constructs. This does not mean that we are trapped in our own private reality, since we do communicate with one another. What is rejected here is the idea of any *universal* criteria. This construct need not be a completely individual thing. It is a social construct, the product of some group. The question then becomes, "*Whose* reality?" and the answer is that the Western construction, the progress myth, has most effectively dominated the globe and has accordingly determined what is true and right. This, however, on postmodern grounds, is, as we have seen, not because it is somehow a more ac-

7. Ibid., p. 31.
8. Ibid., p. 32.
9. Ibid.

curate description of reality. Why, then, has it been accepted? Why does one view rule, with the consequent subjugation or oppression of others? This question has particularly occupied the attention of deconstructionism.

Deconstruction

Jacques Derridá, the French literary critic most frequently considered the originator of deconstruction, has termed the dominant Western intellectual tradition a "metaphysics of presence." There is believed to be a real given that is present in our intellectual system, and that this is before and independent of language and thought about it. Western modernism believes that it so accurately captures and depicts this given that it can be said virtually to reflect it. This is the *mimetic* view of truth, which Derridá and other deconstructionists attack. In their view, there is no possibility of getting to a pre-linguistic and preconceptual "reality." What is claimed to be present is actually absent. The "given" is actually a construct, formed by human discourse.[10]

By exposing this character of the modernist claim to knowledge, the deconstructionists are attempting, not to destroy, but to administer therapy. Like psychotherapists who help the patients recognize their own illusions so that they can move beyond them, deconstructionists try to help late modernity recognize its own illusions, such as naive realism and the correspondence view of truth. What is exposed by their deconstruction is the impulse to oppression and ultimately to violence. The realist metaphysics of presence has a totalizing tendency. It seeks to build a comprehensive scheme, which explains everything. To do this, there has to be some exclusion of elements that do not fit. This is done by repressing those who raise contrary points and erasing the memory of them.[11]

One paradigm example of this is racism, in which there is a totalizing vision of the world based on one's likeness to or difference from, what the racist takes as normal, namely, that which is the same as he or she is. More subtle and more widely accepted is the way immigrants are treated. Anyone who is not a U.S. citizen is considered an *alien*, and the process of becoming a citizen is called *naturaliza-*

---

10. Ibid., p. 33.
11. Ibid., pp. 34–35.

tion, implying that being a citizen is the natural (or normal) state. These new citizens must then find their way into the homogeneity of American life, with their cultural distinctives being dissolved in what has come to be called the "melting pot." This totalizing vision is inherently violent. When a group is convinced of the truth or rightness of its worldview, the only options when encountering those who are different are either totalitarian control or annihilation, according to Kenneth Gergen.[12]

If modernity tried to make homogeneous, "naturalized" persons of us, then the aim of deconstruction is the therapeutic process of "denaturalization." Deconstruction tries to help people see that what seems so natural to them is actually cultural in origin. It attempts to dismantle the totalizing visions that have been used to disenfranchise minorities and open the door for justice.[13]

The effects of deconstruction can be disorienting. This is true, first, because social constructs have been brought into being to shield us from the "abyss of meaninglessness." There is security in having such a shield, and the security derives in part from the belief that this reality is objective, is the way things really are. To be told that this is simply a construct, a fiction of sorts, is disconcerting, to say the least. "An arbitrarily chosen worldview can scarcely function as a worldview anymore. We are left without a buffer against chaos, worldless and disoriented."[14]

Beyond that, however, disorientation results from deconstruction because we come to realize our part in creating that construct. We have, unknowingly and inadvertently in most cases, been guilty of complicity in the violence; we have been involved in the terror. To discover that we have naively shared in the modern dream of progress, the postmodern therapy of deconstruction can be a painful discovery.[15]

Not everyone has encountered deconstruction, however. One of the reasons for this is the hyperreality and the culture of images. This is the fact that in an age heavily dependent on communications technology, there is a "reality" that is not only constructed, but is glorified with hype as "better than the real thing." This is the Disney-

12. Ibid., p. 35.
13. Ibid., p. 36.
14. Ibid., p. 37.
15. Ibid.

world culture, the Cool Whip society. This simulated world is actually numbing. It is seen in politics, where spin doctors manipulate the perception without providing the substance.[16]

Postmodernism has not only deconstructed any metaphysics of presence, however. It has also produced the decentered self. In the modernist scheme, the answer to the question, "Who am I?" is found in the postulate of human autonomy. The very core and basis of the modernist project is the self-centering ego, the independently rational self. Without this, there would be no basis for confidence in the results and achievements of modern science. This conception has produced liberal democracy. Beyond that, however, it is the imperial self of the acquisitive conqueror and pioneer. This lies behind the hegemony of Western colonialism. The free and autonomous subject uses this freedom to master the world of nonhuman or subhuman objects. It is this process of conquest and mastery that gives this self its identity.[17]

We have seen the postmodern deconstruction of epistemological optimism. The same is true of the postmodern treatment of anthropological self-assurance. There are two reasons for the demise of this understanding of the self. The first is that, when left unrestrained, the autonomous self always expresses itself in violence. It despoils the natural environment, as we have seen in the environmental crisis. It also, however, exploits and terrorizes other humans: women, minorities, aboriginal peoples, and others.[18] Beyond that, however, this understanding of the self, when believed and acted on, also leads to a rebounding on itself. The massive bureaucracies and economic structures created to produce the desired progress prove stifling. The modern self finds itself being managed, rather than being the manager, conquered by the socioeconomic systems of modernity.[19]

The second reason for the shaking of anthropological self-assurance is that postmodern thought has come to realize that this understanding of the self is also a construct, a fiction, a modern invention. And this also means that rather than the human being the autonomous self that takes language and uses it for its own purposes, language is seen as shaping the self. The downside of this development

16. Ibid., pp. 38–39.
17. Ibid., pp. 48–49.
18. Ibid., p. 49.
19. Ibid., p. 50.

is that when one realizes that the autonomous self is a fiction, one is thrown into doubt about all previous beliefs about humanness and all the courses of action that those beliefs sustained.[20]

Incredulity about Metanarratives

It is not merely reality that is not what it used to be. The same is true for history. Modernism has given metanarratives—grand, arching explanations of the whole of history. This was the belief that there was a pattern, of which history was the unfolding. The large-scale interpretations of history were universal in their application. This might be the modern belief in progress, the Christian teaching of redemptive history in Jesus Christ, or the dialectical materialism that was communism's philosophy of history. These metanarratives tied all the facts of history into a neat package. Philosopher Alisdair MacIntyre (not a postmodernist) has reinterpreted ethics on the basis of story as historically and culturally conditioned, rather than as universal systems of principles, to be discovered, understood, and applied.[21] Metanarratives go beyond this, claiming to be universal. This confident project has failed, however, just as the ideas of metaphysics of presence and the autonomous self. It has failed, first, because it is epistemologically impossible to know all of history in sufficient detail to be able to make these grand schemes.[22] Further, metanarratives, because of their totalizing character, have also been the means of oppression. Postmodernism sees these metanarratives as constructs, just as genuinely as metaphysics of presence and the centered self.[23]

Middleton and Walsh are not totally uncritical of postmodernism. They raise a number of objections to this movement:

1. While totalization and violence are definitely undesirable, it does not seem to them to be obvious that metanarratives have been the exclusive sources of such. This is also sometimes true of more local narratives. They give as an example the situation of "ethnic cleansing" in the Balkan states, where the modernist metanarrative of Marxism actually held those tendencies in check. People seem in-

20. Ibid., pp. 50–51.
21. Ibid., pp. 66–68.
22. Ibid., p. 70.
23. Ibid., p. 71.

herently to need metanarratives, so local narratives may come to be treated as if they were metanarratives.[24]

2. Postmodernism, for all of its criticism of metanarratives, especially modern metanarratives, is actually something of a metanarrative itself. Postmodernism is therefore caught in what Middleton and Walsh call a "performative contradiction," arguing against the necessity of metanarratives by surreptitiously appealing to a metanarrative of its own.[25]

Nor are Middleton and Walsh completely certain of the relationship of postmodernity to modernity. They acknowledge that in their discussion of hyperreality, they have alternated between the use of the terms "postmodern" and "late modern." This is because we are in a period of cultural transition, where genuinely novel features coexist side by side with continued, even heightened, central features of the older period and philosophy. This is especially true of the emphasis on human autonomy.[26]

Similarly, in their discussion of the decentered self, they raise the question of whether postmodernism should here be called hypermodern, thus echoing Thomas Oden's observation. They note that in that construction the constructed self utilizes the best of modern technology. Conversely, the use of such technology requires the assumption of the malleability of the self. They conclude, "On the level of socioeconomic analysis this would seem to indicate that postmodernity is little more than a logical extension of the culture of capitalism."[27]

The Biblical Answer

The strategy of the second half of Middleton and Walsh's book is to give an exposition of the Christian answer to the challenge of postmodernity. The real question, they say, is this: "Does the Christian faith have the resources to face the postmodern challenge, withstand it, even learn from it?"[28] Although they are critical of postmodernism at certain points, they accept the legitimacy of its concern about the oppressive use of metanarratives. More specifically, therefore,

24. Ibid., pp. 75–76.
25. Ibid., pp. 76–77.
26. Ibid., p. 41.
27. Ibid., pp. 54–55.
28. Ibid., p. 81.

they ask, "Does the postmodern suspicion of metanarratives apply, legitimately, to the biblical story? Are we required, in the name of justice and compassion, to give up the biblical metanarrative and opt for a merely local tale?"[29]

Middleton and Walsh grant that there is some basis, both from a systematic insight and a historical observation, for the postmodern suspicion of metanarratives. The former stems from the fact that those who develop and set forth metanarratives and worldviews are finite human beings. They are therefore incapable of gathering all the data necessary to create a total view, but beyond that, being sinful, they will inevitably tend to use such ideologies for their own purposes, which results in oppression of others. The historical observation is simply that in fact the biblical story has been used to oppress and exclude those regarded as infidels and heretics. It is used to rationalize or legitimate one group's activities, which may include prejudice and violence.[30]

Their conclusion in the transition to discussion of the biblical metanarrative is that metanarratives can be used either for oppression and violence or for justice and healing. "The important question, then, would not be *whether* the Christian faith is rooted in a metanarrative, but *what sort of* metanarrative the Scripture contains."[31]

The strategy employed in examining the biblical story is to show that, negatively, it does not endorse or support the oppression that has sometimes been associated with it, and that positively, it sets forth a justification for concern about the oppressed. Middleton and Walsh begin their consideration with the biblical story of the exodus from Egypt and Israel's subsequent constitution as a people on Mount Sinai. They do this because Jews regard this as the central and founding event of their own narrative, and Christians also regard it as the central event of the Old Testament. Also impressive are the numerous retellings of the story throughout the Bible, in such diverse texts as Deuteronomy 26:1–11; Joshua 24, and Psalms 105 and 106.[32]

The exodus event had a profound ethical meaning for Israel and it also does for us. For later Israel, the answer to the question, What

29. Ibid., p. 83.
30. Ibid., pp. 83–84.
31. Ibid., p. 84.
32. Ibid., pp. 88–91.

am I to do? followed upon answering a prior question, Of what story am I a part? And what was the nature of the ethical action? Because this story reminded them of the oppressive suffering they had experienced, it created in them a sensitivity to suffering. One might even regard this motif as the central thrust of the exodus, according to Middleton and Walsh:

> What has become clear in recent biblical scholarship, especially since the ground-breaking sociological study of Norman Gottwald, is that the whole purpose of the exodus-Sinai event was for Yahweh to found a community with an ethical pattern of life alternative to that of imperial Egypt. Because of the distinctive ongoing story it told, remembered, and participated in, this was to be a community which refused to cause oppression and instead was committed to fostering justice and compassion toward the marginal.[33]

It was the prophets who most fully articulated this theme of justice, as they retold the story of the exodus. They did this both in their criticism of Israel's later history, especially the corrupt monarchy, and in their promise of an eschatological future. The difficulty was that, rather than following the exodus story, the people of Israel had become involved in the Canaanite Baal story of cyclical fertility and guaranteed security. Because Yahweh was against all injustice, whether Egyptian or Israelite, he threatened that they would again be taken into bondage, in the Babylonian captivity. This indeed happened, and caused the people to call out to God once again. The prophets then made it clear that God's purpose was not simply that Israel be set up as a nation that practiced justice, but that "Israel's distinctive practice of justice was to shine as a beacon in the ancient Near East, attracting other nations to the distinctive God who wills such practice."[34] The people of Israel discovered that Yahweh was not simply their God, but the creator of the entire heaven and earth, with a redemptive purpose for all peoples. But this purpose was not merely for all peoples alive at that time, but extends even to us: "the

33. Ibid., p. 94.
34. Middleton and Walsh, "Facing the Postmodern Scalpel: Can the Christian Faith Withstand Deconstruction?" in *Apologetics in the Postmodern World*, ed. Timothy R. Phillips and Dennis L. Okholm (Downers Grove, Ill.: InterVarsity, 1995), p. 147.

biblical God has an overarching narrative purpose alternative to the many oppressive systems and stories in which we find ourselves."[35]

Even the shape of the canon reflects this concern. Middleton and Walsh follow James Sanders' understanding of the canon, which calls attention to the fact that the Torah, the founding story, ends with Deuteronomy, not with Joshua. It ends with the people outside the promised land. This is indicative that only a Torah that excludes the land settlement could have been meaningful for the people in the exile. It was the retelling of the story in a form that was meaningful for landless exiles. Further, the story begins with the account of creation. This was further indication that God's purposes extended to all people.[36]

Jesus' ministry was also anti-totalizing. He avoided any discussion of holiness, probably because this had been made a means of superiority and oppression. Further, he repeatedly sided with the marginal. His act of cleansing the temple is one dramatic instance. And in the crucifixion he recapitulated the story of Israel, the suffering of the prophets and of exilic Israel. He embraced marginality and pain, thus bearing the sins of the world.[37]

The conclusion of this entire argument is clear and definite:

> The biblical metanarrative thus addresses our postmodern situation with both compassion and power. But does this metanarrative escape the postmodern charge of totalization and violence? On our analysis, it does far more than that. Far from promoting violence, the story the Scriptures tell contains the resources to shatter totalizing readings, to convert the reader, to align us with God's purposes of shalom, compassion and justice.[38]

This is more than an apologetic concern, however. It is not simply a matter of giving an answer to the charges brought against Christianity and its metanarrative. We must submit ourselves to the biblical text, allowing it to judge and convert us. The charge of totalization against Christianity can best be answered by concrete, nontotalized lives of individual Christians. The point of telling the

35. *Truth Is Stranger*, p. 102.
36. Ibid., pp. 99–100.
37. Ibid., pp. 102–5.
38. Ibid., p. 107.

biblical story is to contribute to the empowerment of the church in its mission in the postmodern world.[39]

The Self

The validity and pertinence of the biblical metanarrative are not restricted to seeing that it does not lead to oppressive totalization, however. It also speaks to the problem of the decentered self. Actually, there is a tension in the postmodern understanding of self. The postmodern self is both postmodern and hypermodern. It fluctuates between a new form of autonomy and an experience of victimization. Middleton and Walsh call this the "dialectic of tyrant and victim."[40] The biblical narrative, however, gives an alternative to both tendencies, teaching that humanity was created in the image of God.

This image is understood functionally, in terms both of Genesis 1 and Psalm 8. That is to say, rather than focusing on something substantive or structural in the human, the image is construed as the exercise of God's rule on his behalf. Even in exile, humans are God's representatives to exercise power, agency, and responsibility on earth.[41] Special indication of this is found in the fact that God created for six days, and then rested on the seventh. We are in that seventh day, and the reason God is able to rest is because we now carry on his task of ruling over the creation.[42] We are not merely victims, whether of the exile and captivity, or of postmodern fragmentation.

This aspect of the image of God speaks to the victimization problem, but what about the other, the autonomy problem? Cannot this ruling function become a matter of oppression? In fact, some, such as Lynn White, have attributed the ecological problem to this very teaching of Christianity.[43] A close look at the biblical story shows that this is not the case. "The true purpose of human imaging is not to control and disempower others but to mediate

---

39. Ibid.
40. Ibid., p. 109.
41. Ibid., p. 121.
42. Ibid., p. 123.
43. White's lecture, delivered in Washington, D.C., December 26, 1966, is reproduced in the appendix to Francis Schaeffer, *Pollution and the Death of Man: The Christian View of Ecology* (Wheaton, Ill.: Tyndale, 1970), pp. 70–85.

God's blessing and enhance the life and well-being of all creatures, *just as God did in creating the world*. . . . Humans, as the *image and likeness* of this God, are to use their power and rule for the benefit of others."[44]

If humans are to rule the earth with loving nurture rather than oppressive control, this is also true of the relationship of humans to other humans. Middleton and Walsh point out that in the creation account, in which the humans (both male and female) are commissioned to rule the earth, there is no reference to ruling over other humans.[45] The brutality that follows the fall, such as Cain's murder of Abel, comes only because there has been a disruption of the original creation.[46] Further, Jesus, by not grasping for glory and power, but by submitting himself to the futility of death, has reversed the problematic situation of the human race.[47]

Middleton and Walsh now undertake to answer the first question, "Where are we?" The postmodern has a profound sense of homelessness in this world, for three reasons. First is the realization that this world is our own social construction. Second, there is the guilt and embarassment that come from the realization that we have used our constructions to oppress other people. Third, there is the awareness that because we have polluted it, the world has become not only inhospitable but downright threatening to humans remaining at home within it.[48]

Our authors develop their response to this problem in several ways. First, they show that the creation is "an extravagant and eloquent gift of the Creator." This is in contrast to the modern understanding, in which realism, by mastering nature, has rendered it silent. And the postmodern concern for hearing the voice of the other has not been extended to the nonhuman other. In the biblical view, however, God "calls" the creation into existence, and it comes to be by responding to that call. The relationship between God and the creation is that of covenant. Not only is the creation bound to the Creator, but the Creator has bound himself to the creation. This is seen in the fact that in the postflood passage of Genesis 9:9–17, God

44. *Truth Is Stranger*, p. 124.
45. Ibid.
46. Ibid., p. 126.
47. Ibid., p. 137.
48. Ibid., p. 146.

says—no fewer than seven times—that the covenant is not only with humans, but with the entire creation.[49]

Further, the biblical picture of creation shows that it is good. Rather than a threat to humanity that must be forcefully mastered, the creation is fundamentally good. It is created to be a home to humanity. All violence is seen as an intruder into God's good creation.[50]

The biblical story speaks to the postmodern sense of anomie, of homelessness. The only order that can overcome this is an order of redemption. Only in a covenantal context could people raise some sort of protest and ask God to intervene to rectify the disorder of the world.[51]

The question of epistemology must be addressed. In terms of the story about the three umpires, Middleton and Walsh come closest to the second, with what they call "epistemological stewardship." The idea that the creation is a given, prior to our knowing it, and that it is a gift from God affirms the element of truth in the realist view. Part of our call as God's stewards is to know the world. This, however, must be understood in light of the fact that our knowledge is a construct, so that knowledge is perspectival. While some have steered a middle course by what they term "critical realism," Middleton and Walsh decline to use that term because it still carries overtones of the desire to "get it right." By epistemological stewardship they refer to the idea that there is a covenant, not only between God and us and God and the rest of the creation, but between us and the rest of the creation. Rather than engaging the world as masters, an epistemology of love calls for engaging reality as image-bearing rulers.[52]

What, then, is the Christian and biblical solution to the problems that have been posed? Middleton and Walsh propose not merely a theoretical solution, an explanation of what should happen, but a practical solution, a program that would alter the world.

The authors propose that what is needed as a counter to the disorientation that is abroad is a reorientation, a return to our biblical roots. How is this to be done, however? Since we have been shaped by a variety of cultural factors, how do we form a distinctively biblical way of life? One approach, used for centuries, is the approach

49. Ibid., pp. 147–48.
50. Ibid., pp. 153–54.
51. Ibid., pp. 164–65.
52. Ibid., pp. 167–69.

of "apologetics" or "contextualization." This is pictured as taking the essential message of Scripture and applying it to or correlating it with the present situation. All these approaches have a common assumption: that someone can stand *outside* the Christian faith and the contemporary situation, in order to correlate the two. This, however, is a modernist conception, which fails to come to grips with the fact that there is no neutral place to stand. Rather, "interpretation, we have come to realize, is intrinsically tradition-dependent."[53]

A more honest and postmodern understanding of what living the Christian faith authentically in our contemporary culture involves is required. This, Middleton and Walsh propose, is best done by "indwelling" or "inhabiting" the story. This, in fact, is what faith really is: "Biblical faith is not abstract, contextless or timeless but is a personal and communal response to what God has done in the story."[54]

What is involved in indwelling the story, however, is to indwell it as canonical and normative. Walter Brueggemann is right: we are not so much called to interpret or apply it, but to submit our experience to it. When we do this, however, we find that the biblical text has an odd angularity to it. One way in which this can be handled is to reduce the Bible to a series of generalized theological ideas. This is not the approach to be followed, however, for "the transformative power of the Scriptures is precisely their ability to challenge us by the odd things they actually assert and narrate about God, the world, and ourselves."[55]

This angularity is clearly seen in what Phyllis Trible calls "texts of terror." These are passages where women, in particular, are victims of violence and brutality, of which neither the primary characters in the plot nor the biblical authors or editors seem to register any disapproval, and either explicitly or implicitly seem to approve. Among these are the banishment of Hagar, the rape of Tamar, the gang rape of an unnamed concubine, and Jephthah's sacrifice of his daughter to fulfil a vow.[56]

These texts present a problem because they seem to contradict the claim that the Bible is anti-totalizing or counterideological. This is a problem not simply as an objection coming from the outside, but for

53. Ibid., p. 174.
54. Ibid.
55. Ibid., p. 175.
56. Ibid., pp. 176–77.

us as Christians. There are several possible responses to this problem. One is simply to swallow our objections and submit to the Bible's authority. Another is to employ hermeneutical method to explain away the problems, contending that they do not exist in Scripture, but only in our understanding of it. Yet another option is simply to reject the Bible as being subethical and oppressive, either abandoning the faith completely or continuing to hold it, but on some other grounds than the Bible. None of these approaches is satisfactory, however, Middleton and Walsh assert, because they never really deal with the question of why these texts of terror were included in the biblical canon.[57]

Once again, Middleton and Walsh follow Brueggemann's explanation: these texts have been introduced and retained as a dissenting counterexperience to the overall account of God's acts. "They function, in other words," say our authors, "as an inner-biblical critique of any totalizing or triumphalistic reading of the metanarrative."[58] They are retained and included as a corrective, to prevent the employment of the biblical metanarrative in oppressive ways.[59]

Trible's exposition of the texts of terror gives us some guidance at this point. She makes clear that each of these texts cries out for resolution. Yet this is a resolution that will have to occur outside the biblical text. The Bible is an open-ended book. It calls us to live within its story, and to continue it: "Far from being a closed book about a story that has ended, the Bible authorizes our faithful enactment of the Author's purposes precisely in order to continue the story across the pages of history."[60] Middleton and Walsh introduce the idea of an uncompleted Shakespearean stage play. It would not be satisfactory either to perform it in the incomplete form, or to add a conclusion to it. What should be done is to gather a group of highly trained, sensitive, and experienced Shakespearean actors and have them improvise a fifth act for themselves. This improvisation would, however, have to be faithful to the portion of the script that was possessed.[61]

This is what we, as postmodern Christians, are called to do. We are to live the drama, thoroughly immersed in it, in a fashion consis-

57. Ibid., pp. 178–79.
58. Ibid., p. 179.
59. Ibid., p. 180.
60. Ibid., p. 182.
61. Ibid., pp. 182–83.

tent with it. Thus, we are not simply to follow it as if it were a rule-book, but to improvise. Yet we are not left without any guidance. For we have access to the Author of the story, who has given us his Spirit to dwell within us and to guide us. This avoids both the difficulty that the past portion of the story does not necessarily address the specific world in which we live, and the risk of perpetuating the same sorts of oppression and violence that are described in the texts of terror.[62]

Middleton and Walsh contend that alongside the two biblical motifs of sensitivity to suffering and the creative intention of the author that characterize the biblical story, there is another dimension that needs to be kept in mind: the open-endedness of the biblical text. We are called to continue the story. We are called to "contribute to plot resolution in a future that is genuinely unscripted."[63] Middleton and Walsh see the present cultural pain and confusion as God's doing, as his judgment on modernity, much like the curse of Babel. There is strong resemblance between the predicament of people today and that of the tower-builders of Babel. People today do not "hear" one another, and are fragmented and scattered. Both curses were redressed at Pentecost. It is as if we are viewing and are part of a drama, in which Act IV was the life of Jesus and Act V the story of the church. Yet this act is unfinished, like the uncompleted Shakespearean play. Our task and our opportunity are to enter the drama and continue it by living it out. Only thus will the full result of Pentecost's reversal of Babel be effective.[64]

Analytical Summary

We can tie together the strands of this proposal by making several analytical and interpretive observations.

1. Middleton and Walsh take seriously the postmodern challenge. They believe that the modern period is dead, or at least dying, and that postmodernity is taking its place and must be dealt with. While not totally uncritical of postmodernity, they basically accept its criticisms of naive realism, a correspondence theory of truth, and totalizing metanarratives.

---

62. Ibid., p. 184.
63. Ibid., p. 187.
64. Ibid., pp. 189–95.

They acknowledge the presence of oppression and grant that the Christian faith has sometimes been used this way.

2. Middleton and Walsh believe that Christianity, when properly understood, not only does not justify the oppression that postmodernism decries, but offers a solution for the cultural confusion in which our society finds itself.

3. Middleton and Walsh's approach to the Bible is to treat it as narrative. Its truth is not in the timeless propositions it contains, but in the story that it tells. That story affects even the canonical shape of the text.

4. Not all that appears in the Bible is to be taken as normative. In particular, certain "texts of terror" that depict oppression of powerless persons are to be seen, not as justifying totalizing use of metanarrative, but as a protest against such practice.

5. We are called to enter into the biblical drama, living as participants in the sensitivity to suffering and the creative intention of God. The biblical story is to be considered an unfinished drama, however, of which we are to be contributors by continuing to write the plot by living out our lives.

6. The God described in Middleton and Walsh's book is very similar to that propounded by the "free will theists" or "openness of God" theologians. He partners with humans, allows them free will, does not overwhelm them, and responds to their actions.

Evaluation

This is a position that provokes thought and reaction. It has some very salutary features, but also some significant shortcomings.

Positive

1. Middleton and Walsh have correctly understood much of the thrust of postmodernism. They realize that a major cultural change is taking place, and cannot be ignored or treated by using the old arguments that fit an earlier way of thinking.

2. Middleton and Walsh have made a genuine effort to be Christian and biblical, to show the relevance of Christianity to the cultural crises of the day. They have taken seriously the biblical motifs and desire to let them judge us.

3. Middleton and Walsh's understanding of Christianity is more than a system of thought; it is a total matter of life, in keeping with the biblical conception. The Bible is indeed a story of God's plan and its unfolding.

4. Middleton and Walsh have correctly seen and acknowledged that Christianity has sometimes functioned in an imperialistic fashion, regarding all other views as erroneous and to be overcome, sometimes without due regard for the means employed.

5. Middleton and Walsh have correctly heeded the biblical injunctions to integrity, justice, and the like. This plays a more prominent part in the biblical message than Christians have sometimes recognized.

6. Middleton and Walsh confess a willingness to let the Bible pass judgment on the interpreter and all schemes of ideology, rather than themselves sitting in judgment on it and making it conform to their preconceptions.

Negative

1. There is something of an oversimplification, both of Middleton and Walsh's understanding of postmodernism and of the relationship between postmodernism and modernism. They tend to see modernism as completely passé, whereas in fields of science and even in some ministry styles (which engage in "ecclesiastical engineering") it is very much alive. Similarly, they seem to be ambivalent regarding the extent to which postmodernity is a contradiction to modernity and the extent to which it is actually an extension (and, perhaps, exaggeration) of modernity. Although they mention this possibility, that postmodernity is actually late modernity or hypermodernity, they do not follow up on these hints or clues.

2. Middleton and Walsh are critical of postmodernity at certain points, but do not come to grips with the contradictions involved in its tendency to become its own metanarrative. Oppression is not the exclusive possession of modernism. Some of the greatest intolerance that can be encountered today is in postmodern settings, as anyone who has ever experienced the sting of the political correctness movement can testify. This may be inherent in postmodernism. If realism, foundationalism, and a correspondence view of truth are abandoned, one would expect that the result would be a pluralism, with its consequent tolerance of various differing ideologies. Instead,

however, differences cannot be mediated by appeal to some universal standards or data. What happens, when one's own view is to be maintained, is that differing voices must be suppressed. Allan Bloom was correct in his description of certain aspects of the *closing* of the American mind.[65]

Similarly, there is a lack of critical appraisal of the presuppositions of postmodernity. One thing that should emerge from realizing that viewpoints are perspectival would be that this applies to one's own view. This does not seem to be present, in many cases, however. If postmodernity is correct, then, of course, it is relative.

The status of postmodernity is unclear in Middleton and Walsh's discussion. Is it merely another stage in the development of culture, to be replaced at some point in the future? Or is it somehow the final step? If it is the former, then it must be regarded with considerable tentativity. Given the accelerating pace of change, culturally and intellectually, it is to be expected that the lifespan of postmodernism will be considerably shorter than that of modernism. Indeed, some of us think that we are already beginning to see the first glimmers of what will be the dawn of the next age, that of postpostmodernity. There seems to be in Middleton and Walsh's discussion something of a finality about postmodernity.

In part, there appears to be something of the "chronological snobbery" that assumes that what is more recent is superior to what is older. If this is the case, then this appears to involve the progress concept, which is part and parcel of the modern view. In other words, one should be postmodern because this is a later advance over the earlier, modern, view. But if that is the case, then the modern view, including the progress factor, is false. There seems to be an inherently contradictory stance here.

3. There is a powerful commitment to the postmodern position that becomes a controlling factor in the theology. Thus, the criterion used to sift the genuine from the spurious in the biblical story is postmodernity, especially the critique of oppression. This begins to sound as if postmodernity is functioning as a metanarrative. But if that is the case, then it is subject to its own criticism of metanarratives. As with some other postmodern philosophies and theologies,

65. Allan Bloom, *The Closing of the American Mind: How Higher Education Has Failed Democracy and Impoverished the Souls of Today's Students* (New York: Simon & Schuster, 1987).

that of Middleton and Walsh appears to be in serious need of being deconstructed. If deconstruction is true (and if it is a metanarrative of sorts), then it applies to every ideology, including deconstruction.

Everyone works from some perspective or presuppositions. Thus, Middleton and Walsh should be more honest about their presuppositions, which are clearly present. The influence of existentialism is visible at a number of points, including the view of freedom, the objection to a closed system, and so on.

4. These men do not address the question of whether their discussion of postmodernity versus modernity is itself postmodern or modern. This is part of a larger question that needs to be asked: Within what paradigm is one functioning when one discusses paradigm shifts? That issue is not addressed. Middleton and Walsh simply proceed as if they were on some neutral ground. In a truly postmodern context, however, that is not possible.

5. Middleton and Walsh do not make clear what view of truth they are employing. If correspondence is illicit, what form of truth is this? It appears that they are working with some sort of pragmatic view of truth, but this deserves some clear exposition. At times, they seem to slip back into a virtual correspondence view, especially when discussing the biblical tradition.

6. There are a number of problems with Middleton and Walsh's employment of the biblical tradition. For one thing, despite their professed desire to let the biblical story judge the interpreter rather than vice versa, the postmodern opposition to metanarratives and oppression is used as the criterion by which Scripture is employed. They acknowledge the possible charge of a canon within the canon, but do not really respond fully to it.

The nature of the authority of the Bible is not clear. The open-endedness of the biblical story, and the suggestion that we are to write and live the final act, calls into question the uniqueness of canonicity.

Although Middleton and Walsh presumably would identify themselves as evangelicals, the sources on whom they rely for their interpretation of the biblical story (Brueggemann, Gottwald, Trible, etc.) certainly do not hold what is usually considered an evangelical understanding of Scripture. There is therefore considerable basis for expecting either distortion of the evangelical understanding of the story, or contradiction between it and the presuppositions brought to the Bible.

7. A parallel to this latter problem can be seen with respect to Middleton and Walsh's understanding of the goal of the biblical narrative. This seems to be primarily oriented toward the achievement of social justice, or something of the sort. Just *how* individuals become changed is not equally clear. Evangelicalism, in whatever form, has usually emphasized regeneration. There is a strange silence on that topic.

8. The status of Christianity, or of the biblical story, is not clear. Is this *the* truth, *a* truth, or *our* (i.e., the community's) truth? What is the status of other religions, which on the surface at least, appear to be in contradiction to biblical Christianity?

7

De/con/structive Evangelicalism

B. Keith Putt

A decade ago, Wheaton College English professor Roger Lundin predicted a time when evangelicals would adopt and utilize deconstruction in doing their theology.[1] He wrote this after spending a summer in a seminar studying deconstruction. He saw this development resulting from what he termed the "evangelical lag"—the tendency to reject something, but then eventually to adopt it. As unlikely as such an occurrence may have seemed at the time, it appears that Lundin's prophecy has already been fulfilled. Although several evangelicals may be utilizing deconstruction in their theologizing, probably the clearest instance of this is found in the thought of Billy Keith Putt, associate professor of philosophy of religion at Southwestern Baptist Theological Seminary since 1990.

Putt is unknown outside the school in which he teaches, because he is not a publishing scholar. His published materials during a decade of teaching consist of a single book chapter, one journal article, and a handful of short book reviews. His thought must largely be derived from his dissertations and two unpublished papers.

Reading Putt, one is immediately struck by the deconstructionist feel or mood of his writing and thought. Whether the content is actually that of deconstruction, the style definitely is. The use of punning, slashes, overstrikes, parentheses, and other devices is reminis-

---

1. Roger Lundin, "Deconstructive Therapy," *Reformed Journal* 36.1 (January 1986): 15–16.

cent of the writing of Mark C. Taylor.[2] There is an intuitive, immediate presentation of images, rather than the cool, rational analysis that was customary for so long in twentieth-century philosophy. To draw a parallel (stylistically only) to the Death of God movement of the 1960s, Putt's thought and writing is much more like that of Thomas J. J. Altizer than it is like that of the linguistic analyst, Paul van Buren.

The Modern Approach to Knowledge

Putt uses the analogy of navigation to describe the human predicament and show the former and current means of dealing with it. He pictures human beings as adrift on the "infinite sea of being." In these unfamiliar and treacherous waters, humans try to navigate by shooting the stars, trying to get a fix on their location.[3]

Traditionally, reason is the means used to do such plotting and navigating. For Descartes, reason could map out the points along the route. Such Cartesian cartography offers "the security of exact location: self, God, and world are clearly marked, and if one remains on a logical course, one can move from one point to the next without fear of shipwreck or of wa(o)ndering aimlessly."[4] The individual may thus p(i)lot out one's existence and reach the destination.

Putt recognizes two familiar forms of the modern quest for certainty: the rationalist path of Descartes, with its confidence in clear and distinct ideas; and the empiricist trust in perceptual data.[5] Putt characterizes modern thinking with these two pure forms of Enlightenment thought: the rationalism of Descartes and the empiricism of Locke and Hume. He does not endeavor to distinguish less thoroughgoing forms of modern thought.

This quest for certainty also shows itself in hermeneutical theory. The first question in hermeneutics, says Putt, is the question of what

2. For example, he uses "G⊗d" to distinguish his understanding of God from the philosophical God of ontotheology.
3. B. Keith Putt, "The Inescapable Fragrance of Flesh: John Caputo's Anti-ethical Ethics of Obligation," paper presented at the annual meeting of the Southwest Commission on Religious Studies, Dallas, March 12, 1991, p. 1; "The Kingdom of God as a Sacred Christ(an)archy: A Suggested Postmodern Biblical Ethic," Ph.D. colloquium paper, Southwestern Baptist Theological Seminary, Fort Worth, February 21, 1995, p. 1.
4. Ibid.
5. "Deconstructing the (Non)being of G⊗D: A Trinitarian Critique of Postmodern A/theology," (Ph.D. diss., Rice University, May 1995), p. 6.

comes first, or the starting point. The search for some nonhermeneutical starting point is an indication of modernity's desire for certainty. There is a fear that unless some such starting point is discovered, meaning will be destroyed in the "bottomless pit of indeterminacy," for there is no neutral point from which to judge among various interpretations. The crucial question is, "Does the question of truth demand that the question of beginning lead to a nonhermeneutical, objective, and verifiably certain ground for all knowledge?"[6]

The search for epistemological certainty has been carried on from at least as early as the time of Plato. The principle behind Plato's anamnesis—the idea that knowledge is discovering or remembering what one already has innate within one—is that knowledge is the necessary precondition for knowledge. One moves from a prioris to subsequent knowledge in linear fashion. This can be pursued in both directions, however: not only forward to additional truth, but backward to the foundations for knowledge. This, then, is foundationalism: "One can undertake an epistemological archaeology, and 'dig' back through the layers until one can discover a bedrock of first principles (*archai*) upon which the edifice of learning rests. Only if such a beginning can be located can there be any hope for establishing objective and certain truth."[7]

If Plato's approach was premodern, Descartes' was the classical modern form of the quest for certainty. Although a different form, this also is classical foundationalism: "the notion that some ahistorical, immutable, objective, and verifiable substructure for knowledge is the only guarantee of rationality and truth."[8] Because Descartes identifies truth with certainty, he begins with that which he cannot possibly doubt—his own existence: "If, indeed, there are no first principles (*archai*) establishing knowledge, then only epistemological an-*archy* reigns."[9]

This concern for certainty and consequent anxiety in its absence is not merely a matter of epistemology, but also of religion and ethics. This is what Richard Bernstein calls "Cartesian Anxiety," the

6. Putt, "Preunderstanding and the Hermeneutical Spiral," in *Biblical Hermeneutics: A Comprehensive Introduction to Interpreting Scripture*, ed. Bruce Corley, Steve Lemke, and Grant Lovejoy (Nashville: Broadman & Holman, 1966), pp. 203–4.
7. Ibid., p. 204.
8. Ibid.
9. Ibid., p. 205.

disjunction: either knowledge rests on objectively certain grounds, or it is always subject to skepticism. Such an approach has sought to place human existence and reasoning in a linear process, beginning at a purely objective, value-free, disinterested point.[10] This is where theology and biblical interpretation have traditionally begun in the approach of modernity.

The Postmodern Critique

This modern approach has, however, in Putt's judgment, clearly given way to an alternative. In the analogy with which we opened this discussion, he says that there has developed, in recent philosophy, a "plot against such plotting, the recognition that the seas are not smooth, the maps are not as trustworthy, and the stars are not always visible."[11] The problem lies with the faith placed in reason to guarantee navigational success. Reason not only shoots the stars, that is, discovers location, but "shoots for the stars." It "claims to be able to reach them, to view existence from their astronomical heights, and to join them in illuminating the expedition." Postmodern pilots, on the other hand, realize that the stars cannot be reached, that is, obtain absolute certainty. Putt says, "Lying at the heart of postmodern theories of existence is the 'stark refusal to cultivate a nostalgia for the unattainable.'"[12] Because one cannot get off the seas, navigation is always done under these limitations. But the stars are not only unattainable. Sometimes they are misleading—"hiding stars, leaving one in the dark, without sight or site."[13]

The aversion to any sort of totalizing systematization of truth appears early in Putt's writing. In his 1985 dissertation on Paul Ricoeur, he insists that the complexities, or as he terms them, the "ironies" of existence, prevent one from forming a closed system, from being able to claim to have the ultimate meaning of existence: "Religious 'worlds' must remain open; the horizons must constantly be extended; mediation must not end in a dogmatic synthesis."[14]

10. Ibid.
11. "Kingdom of God," p. 1; "Fragrance of Flesh," p. 1.
12. Ibid., p. 2.
13. Ibid.
14. "The Constructive Possibilities of Imagination as Prolegomena to Philosophy of Religion" (Ph.D. diss., Southwestern Baptist Theological Seminary, 1985).

Putt's strong aversion to systematization and objectivity comes through emphatically in his characterization of certain types of evangelical apologetics. Note the types of nouns and adjectives he employs. He uses as an example the work of Norman Geisler in which, he says, "the Christian <u>Weltanschauung</u> has deteriorated into a closed, cosmological system that acts as a fortress against all other 'world'-views." By "combining rationalism, scholasticism, and an implicit empiricism with reference to the criterion for truth," such philosophers of religion "have created grandiose contemporary versions of onto-theological apologetic systems." This system "becomes a heteronomous monolith towering above every other 'world'-view" and must be defended against competing ideologies. Such an apologetic replaces dialogue with "the pluralism of modern culture" with confrontation and debate. The results are distasteful to Putt: "The result of this stagnant scholasticism is violence aimed both at the imaginative character of religious texts and the 'conflict of interpretations' that typify all hermeneutics."[15]

If there can be no final and complete Christian worldview, only worldviews, on what basis does one evaluate or validate them? Putt emphasizes consonance with our experience. While not necessarily repudiating a correspondence theory of truth, he asserts its insufficiency: "If the philosopher tries to validate the references of that 'world' to reality using only a correspondent [sic] theory of truth, he/she eventually fails to discover the full truth value of religious texts." He recommends, following Ricoeur, broadening the concept of truth to include "the revealing of the possibilities of human reality." He terms this contribution of Ricoeur "a brilliant reconstruction of religion."[16]

The realization of the plurality of our experience of the world leads Putt to observe that philosophy of religion cannot be what ontotheology has often in the past made it to be: "theistic proofs, rational apologetics, or scholastic <u>Weltanschauungen</u>."[17] Rather, he contends, on the basis of what he believes may be Ricouer's "finest achievement," that "there can be no <u>philosophy</u> of religion—only the <u>philosophizing</u> of religion."[18]

15. Ibid., pp. 215–16.
16. Ibid., pp. 213–14.
17. Ibid., p. 218.
18. Ibid., p. 227.

The Search for a Postmodern Vehicle of Theology

It is apparent that Putt largely accepts this postmodern challenge to what has been called, following Kant, "ontotheology." But if theology cannot be done in the older way, how is it to be done at all? What is needed is a genuinely postmodern way of navigating, to use his figure. John Caputo, whom Putt terms "one of the most prolific and insightful interpreters of the continental philosophical tradition," gives us an alternative approach, "a way of getting around without definite charts."[19] Utilizing not only Caputo's published works but also eleven unpublished papers and personal correspondence, he develops at length Caputo's views.[20] Caputo finds his source of inspiration in the deconstructive philosophy of Jacques Derridá. There are many different interpretations of Derridá, but Caputo's is rather conservative. Some have understood Derridá as denying objective reference to language. Caputo emphasizes that it is the hegemony of reason that Derridá is denying. Derridá does this by showing that reason always excludes someone or something, some contrary voice. It claims power beyond what it actually has. It tries to tie up all the loose ends into a complete system. On this interpretation, Derridá is not affirming subjectivity, but epistemological humility. Thus he opposes "every logocentric effort to arrest the flux by some metaphysical announcement of presence." What Derridá is doing, according to Caputo, is denying any "exclusive transcendental ground."[21] In many ways, Caputo sees the problem as being the hellenizing of metaphysics, ethics, and religion. In fact, in speaking of Jesus, Caputo uses the Hebraic name, Jeshua, rather than the more familiar Jesus.[22]

Putt even sees Jesus as a pioneer and example to us in this matter of deconstruction. He endorses Ricouer's characterization of Jesus' parables: "Through extravagance and the metaphorical twist, Jesus deconstructed the systems of thought prevalent in first-century Israel in order to reorient those structures. If structures are allowed to os-

19. "Fragrance," p. 2. "Kingdom of God," p. 2. Although much of what Putt presents is in the form of an exposition of Caputo's thought, it is apparent that in general he approves of those ideas. Indeed, one of his papers is subtitled, "A Suggested Postmodern Biblical Ethic."
20. "(De)constructing the (Non)being of G⊗d," pp. 488–91.
21. "Fragrance of Flesh," p. 3; "Kingdom of God," p. 3.
22. "Fragrance of Flesh," p. 25, n. 71.

sify, they become idols, closed systems that are apothesized and defended as holy objects."[23]

Metaphysics or ontotheology has been an attempt to give one bearings in the face of the flux of history and nature. It does this by trying to find some point outside the flux from which to take one's bearings. It attempts not simply to slow down the flux, but to stop it, believing that failure to do so would seem to surrender oneself to meaninglessness. Caputo is going to attempt to navigate, but not by eliminating the flux. Rather, says Putt, "Caputo intends on keeping the flux in play, seeking to find order not outside of it but within it, always recognizing that any order is fleeting, constituted, and cannot be privileged as foundational."[24]

What Caputo offers instead of ontotheology as a means of navigating is what he terms "radical hermeneutics." This raises the question of the human condition, but refuses to accept that there is only the play of signifiers. Caputo argues that Derridá is not denying the existence of a nonlinguistic reality, but is simply asserting that humans can get to that reality outside any signifying systems. The "radical" part of the term "radical hermeneutics" derives from the word for root. This implies a "knotted root system," which means with respect to language that textuality complicates referentiality.[25] Derridá, according to Caputo, is not a textual idealist, denying any nonlinguistic reality. Rather, he rejects the idea that signifiers are atoms. The deconstructionist can still raise the question of truth, when seen in light of these qualifications. As Putt states Caputo's view, truth must be "recognized as an effect, not something dropping into the play of textuality from some transcendental beyond."[26] None of the traditional definitions or tests of truth apply, whether correspondence, coherence, or pragmatic. Caputo maintains that the alternatives are not limited to the absolute presence offered by metaphysics and the absolute absence from nihilism. Rather, he says that human beings experience "plenty of presence-as-given-to-us-under-historical-linguistic-constraints," which Putt terms "a fascinating compound synonym for the flux."[27] Rather than irrationalism or confu-

---

23. "Constructive Possibilities of Imagination," p. 210.
24. "Fragrance of Flesh," p. 4; "Kingdom of God," pp. 3–4.
25. "Fragrance of Flesh," p. 5.
26. Ibid., p. 6.
27. Ibid.

sion, deconstruction gives us the desire to keep the debate open. This openness requires readmitting the discussion of what metaphysics has excluded. Deconstruction poses a threat to metaphysics because the latter has always been "agora-phobic, afraid to go outside and encounter otherness."[28]

Caputo, however, will not accept the comfort and warmth that metaphysics claims to offer against the chill of uncertainty. Thus, he calls for a "cold hermeneutics." While his hermeneutics is cold, however, it also has within it a warm heart. This opens up the ethical possibilities inherent in the hermeneutics, for two primary reasons. Community helps deal with the cold flux because "by huddling together, individuals may find the strength needed to cope with the comfortless, star-less nights," as Putt puts it. Within the community, there is distrust of any attempts at totalization and exclusion, of the domination of individuals. It is also an ethics of dissemination, which allows the many voices to join the conversation.[29]

Beyond that, however, Caputo's radical hermeneutics leads to ethics because of Derridá's recent startling statement that there is one thing that cannot be deconstructed, namely, justice. This means that "an ethical dynamic is tacitly operating throughout Derridá's philosophy." Caputo intends to build on that dynamic by working out a deconstructive ethic. This will be ethics done in a very definite and different way, however.[30]

It would not be accurate, therefore, to say that Caputo is proposing ethics as the means for reinstating religion. Actually, he takes a rather strong and unequivocal stand against ethics, by which he means ethics as usually conceived. In that form, ethics has allied itself with metaphysics. It attempts to offer laws and standards, which are general and universal. It attempts to stop the movement of life, to escape the flux, by elevating universal considerations. In this approach, the individual becomes an artifact to use in establishing the law of morality.[31]

What Caputo is proposing is obligation, which is the sensitivity one feels toward the other who calls for help. The word *obligation* actually comes from a Latin verb, *obligare,* meaning to tie together,

28. Ibid., p. 7.
29. Ibid., pp. 9–10.
30. Ibid., p. 11.
31. Ibid., p. 13.

so that obligation is a matter of being bound to a disaster. Unlike the usual understanding of ethics, however, this obligation does not come from above, from some superior force. Rather, it comes from below, from the sphere of plurality and uncertainty. Thus the obligation both recognizes the uncertainty of the call and also prohibits the uncertainty from leading to inactivity. Obligation can never be directed toward any kind of individuals.[32]

Ethics, considered as ethical systems, fails because it does not take into account the "tear" in existence. When metaphysics, and with it, the systematic type of ethics, deals with persons, it does so as body, by which it means the Greek ideal of body. This is the male, active, athletic, healthy body. There is another way to think of the person, however, not as body but as flesh. Flesh is "soft, vulnerable, open to wounding." It is passive, not active. The very word itself derives from the Sanskrit word *ker*, which means "to tear." Flesh "does not organize through intentionality but can be disorganized, torn apart, disfigured, bowed over."[33] When the body suffers, "it is no longer body, but flesh."[34] And obligation, or justice, is becoming involved in the suffering of the other and acting. Putt says, "The rank fragrance of flesh clings to the one who expends resources in order to comfort, bathe, heal, and feed the afflicted and the oppressed."[35]

Putt's Theopassional Theology

Against this background, Putt develops his own postmodern theology, both epistemologically and ontologically.

Authority and Interpretation of Scripture

It is apparent that for Putt the Bible plays an important role in the matter of authority. He has for some time concerned himself with hermeneutics, and contributed a chapter on the role of preunderstanding to a volume co-authored by a number of scholars with past or present connections to Southwestern Seminary.

In contrast to the Cartesian approach, which attempts to found the understanding of the text on some absolute, unqualified perspec-

32. Ibid., pp. 15–16.
33. Ibid., p. 18.
34. Ibid., p. 20.
35. Ibid., p. 22.

tive, in this case, some nonhermeneutical starting point for hermeneutics, contemporary hermeneutics works within a hermeneutical spiral. All interpretation takes place within contexts affected by earlier generations. These traditions supply preunderstandings, transmitted especially through the texts regarded as authoritative in a community. Such a preunderstanding therefore serves as a perspective from which understanding of the texts takes place, so that there is hopefully a spiraling toward a clearer understanding. It is not possible to do completely "objective" interpretation, beginning with some nonhermeneutical starting point and proceeding from that foundation to knowledge. One always starts where one is.[36]

It would be natural to seek to exempt biblical interpretation from this spiral, since "those dynamics result in the disenfranchising of any claim to there being *the* absolute meaning of a biblical passage."[37] Putt makes quite clear that he believes that God has revealed himself, and that the texts of Scripture are the product of divine inspiration. Nonetheless, this inspiration "does not void their also (1) being historical texts developing within certain contexts, (2) being transmitted through a tradition, and (3) having to be read and interpreted by each new generation."[38] The effect of the objectivist treatment of texts as "cold 'objective' documents communicating information that is ahistorical and unrelated to existence, would be to diminish their impact and possibly even to distort the gospel." We should not despair, however, for seeing the contribution of preunderstanding "does not lead to biblical relativism but, instead, to an adventure of faith in which knowledge and truth result from the power of God's Spirit working in history, through language, and out of cultural traditions."[39]

A preunderstanding can be found operating even within the scriptural materials themselves. So, for example, with respect to the relationship of the Old and New Testaments, the writer of the letter to the Hebrews and Jesus in Luke assume that the reader or listener has a certain familiarity with Hebrew history and religion.[40]

In addition, preunderstanding also operates from outside the biblical texts. We all bring to the reading of the text our own experience,

36. "Preunderstanding," pp. 205–6.
37. Ibid., p. 206.
38. Ibid.
39. Ibid.
40. Ibid., p. 207.

and indeed, the entire sum of our lives. Putt cites with approval Geoffrey Turner's observation that these presuppositions include such concepts as "history," "revelation," "miracle," "God," and "humanity." When readers first encounter these concepts in the Bible, their initial understanding of them is in terms of their own prior conceptions.[41] Preunderstandings are not restricted to particular concepts, however. They even extend to such matters as the motivations behind one's encounter with the text. How a reader interprets a text is affected by whether that interest is "historical information, existential consolation, aesthetic appreciation, homiletical creation, or ethical admonition."[42]

All of this means that there is not some objective or absolute knowledge of the meaning of the texts: "There can be no closure to the disclosure of meaning in God's written revelation; there can be no absolute knowledge within the techniques of biblical hermeneutics."[43] An absolute meaning "would be . . . meaning detached from history, language, culture, texts, presuppositions, and communities. This essay has attempted to present the thesis that meaning never floats freely outside of the contexts of all the above."[44] Yet this does not mean that true interpretations cannot be constructed. What Putt is opposing is the arrogance that "claims to have built *the* one, completely integrative interpretive structure." Interpretations may be meaningful and true, but they are not total. This calls for a hermeneutic of suspicion, in which one seeks to question every exegetical perspective. If this is not done, exegesis can easily become eisegesis, as one reads one's own preunderstandings into the text.[45]

What is to prevent the interpretation of Scripture from deteriorating into a multitude of subjective understandings? For one thing, biblical texts set certain restrictions on their interpretation. Consequently, says Putt, "they may have more than one possible meaning, but they do not have an infinite number of meanings." The texts challenge the preunderstandings brought to them.[46]

41. Ibid., pp. 207–8.
42. Ibid., p. 208.
43. Ibid.
44. Ibid.
45. Ibid., p. 209.
46. Ibid., p. 211.

The second factor limiting the subjectivity of interpretation is the fact that it is done within communities. This is appropriate, since the Bible originated through individuals within communities, and was canonized, preserved, and interpreted for centuries by individuals within communities. Even the individual who attempts to function independently of any specific community cannot avoid the fact that he or she has been influenced by theologies, sermons, Sunday school materials, and songs, which reflect the influence of communities of faith.[47]

This is how relativism and subjectivism are overcome, then: by submitting one's interpretation to interaction with other members of the community. Putt says: "By keeping the hermeneutical dialogue going, by listening to the different voices, individuals can allow the spiral to progress toward clearer understanding. . . . one discovers in community the critical awareness that leads to a better comprehension of God's written Word and a genuine encounter with God's self-revelation."[48] Putt sees support for this explanation of interpretation in Peter's statement in 2 Peter 1:20 that "no prophecy of the scripture is of any private interpretation."[49]

The Spirit is the one who leads to knowledge of God through the Scripture by what Putt terms inspir(al)ation, first by inspiring writers, canonizing and preserving the revelation, and guiding interpreters. In this there is a certain indeterminacy, since Jesus said that the Spirit is like the wind that blows from somewhere to somewhere, but without our knowing where those somewheres are. Putt concludes: "Perhaps the indeterminacy of the hermeneutical spiral as it moves from (pre)understanding through interpretation to understanding is another example of the creative uncertainty of the Spirit's working through the procedure, always inspir(al)ing new meaning, new truth, and new life."[50]

It is difficult to interpret Putt's statements in this area. His use of language is imprecise. He seems to use truth, meaning, knowledge, and understanding synonymously. Thus, a statement such as "those dynamics result in the disenfranchising of any claim to there being *the* absolute meaning of a biblical passage"[51] seems to refer to the

47. Ibid.
48. Ibid., p. 212.
49. Ibid.
50. Ibid., p. 213.
51. Ibid., p. 206.

epistemological problem of determining an absolute understanding of that meaning. In more customary usage, however, this would imply not simply that we cannot determine that meaning, but that it does not have an absolute meaning, which is an ontological rather than an epistemological matter.

A second area of imprecision concerns the concept of preunderstanding or presupposition. A rather wide variety of presuppositions seems to be subsumed under this single concept. Preunderstanding refers to something as broad as simply faith. At times it appears to involve a conception about the relationship of the New Testament to the Old. Sometimes it involves definite theological concepts, such as those referred to by Geoffrey Turner. It also refers to methodological presuppositions, as in the reference to Bultmann and the use of the historical method. At yet other times, as in the reference to Philo's hermeneutic, it seems to denote philosophical conceptions. These are usually treated as discrete classes of presupposition.

In discussing the relationship of the Holy Spirit to the ongoing process of interpreting the Bible, Putt's different descriptions do not appear to describe the same occurrence. So, for example, he speaks of how the Holy Spirit is "always inspir(al)ing new meaning, new truth, and new life."[52] A similar statement is, "There can be no closure to the disclosure of meaning in God's written revelation."[53] On the surface of it, this sounds like a neo-orthodox doctrine of Scripture, that revelation is the encounter with God through the Scripture. Presumably, however, with his rather subjective view of truth, he is referring to the Spirit inspir(al)ing new *understanding* of the truth, which is objectively present. Yet his constant criticisms of objective truth, as something free-floating, apart from any particular cultural situation, appear to contradict this view.

The same applies to the question of the locus of meaning. While at times Putt seems to be referring to meaning as objectively within the text, at other times it appears to be a product of the interaction of text and interpreter, as in reader–response criticism.

Perhaps this imprecision is to be expected in a theology that utilizes deconstruction. The emphasis on analysis and clarity of language may be a phenomenon of the modern mentality, which came to its zenith in analytical philosophy. That Putt is aware of this con-

52. Ibid., p. 213.
53. Ibid., p. 208.

nection is revealed in a review in which he wrote of Mark C. Taylor: "Mark Taylor's essay is much more enigmatic since he does not write on deconstruction but actually deconstructs."[54] It does compromise an author's right to claim to have been misunderstood, however, although Derridá himself has paradoxically complained about being misunderstood.[55]

The Doctrine of God

Putt holds to a theopassionist view of God. This is simply, as the name would indicate, an emphasis on the idea of divine suffering. Here he shows considerable affinity with the movement known as "free will theism" or "the openness of God."[56] This surfaces in a rather negative review of D. A. Carson's *How Long, O Lord?* Putt feels that Carson's treatment of theopassionism is a caricature. He states that Carson's writing is from Reformed presuppositions, and would therefore not be attractive to those who do not share these presuppositions. The book would not be an adequate choice for those who want one good book on evil and suffering, but if "readers desire a lengthy pastoral reconstruction from the Calvinist perspective in order to augment a broader library, they could probably do worse than Carson."[57]

This affinity also appears in his chapter on the hermeneutical spiral. Here he chooses as his example of the way in which presuppositions can affect the interpretation of Scripture, Philo's allegorizing methodology. He states that Philo had a very strong view of the inspiration and authority of the Bible, so much so that its words are God's words. When, however, those words conflict with Philo's presuppositions, they are taken allegorically. The particular example that Putt selects is Philo's treatment of the passages that seem to attribute emotions to God. Philo takes these to be instances of God accommodating himself to the intellectual weakness of individuals.

54. Review of "New Dimensions in Philosophical Theology" ed. Carl O. Raschke, in *Southwestern Journal of Theology* 26.1 (Fall 1983): 122.

55. Jacques Derridá, "Limited, Inc., abc," *Glyph* 2 (1977): 162–254. This article was written in response to an eleven-page criticism by John Searle.

56. E.g., Clark Pinnock, Richard Rice, John Sanders, William Hasker, and David Basinger, *The Openness of God: A Biblical Challenge to the Traditional Understanding of God* (Downers Grove, Ill.: InterVarsity, 1994).

57. B. Keith Putt, Review of "How Long, O Lord?" by D. A. Carson, in *Southwestern Journal of Theology* 34.3 (Summer 1992): 52.

Putt says that it is not important whether one accepts Philo's presuppositions or agrees with his interpretation. The important thing is to note the influence of the presuppositions on the interpretation: "Philo's hermeneutics illustrates quite well that the meaning of a biblical passage is in some way influenced by what the exegete brings to the text. In Philo's case, he brings a particular Hellenistic philosophical theology and reads the Bible through the lenses supplied by that preconceived theory. In so doing, he shows the inherent danger in allowing presuppositions to operate uncritically."[58]

It is at the point of emphasis on suffering that deconstruction, or more specifically, Caputo's radical hermeneutics, becomes a resource for postmodern theology. Putt believes that Caputo's approach is consistent with that which he himself intends to offer. Caputo has dehellenized metaphysical theology, opening the way for what Putt terms "a theology that takes seriously the jew/christian economy of salvation."[59] Caputo does not develop the idea of a suffering God or address the idea of Trinity, and rejects the traditional conceptions of incarnation, crucifixion, and resurrection. His treatments of love, suffering, forgiveness, and the kingdom of God do, however, provide interesting possibilities for a biblical theopassionist theology. Putt believes that by "contaminating Caputo with Moltmann" he can perhaps "move past classical theism and postmodern a/theology by the repetition of biblical ideas of divine differentiation, divine immanence, and divine compassion."[60]

The G⊗d that is the centerpiece of Putt's theology, then, is clearly not the timeless, impassible, immutable God. Rather, this G⊗d is open to the flux, entering into the movement of history. He is capable of real suffering and of being affected by suffering and disasters. He is temporal, or at least possesses temporality, "since suffering and loving are not static acts that can be completed in some Eternal Now."[61]

Putt believes that the incarnation and its associated doctrines are the key to this understanding of G⊗d as suffering. At this point he parts company with Caputo, who holds that Jesus was a good man, not a God/man. Caputo believes that the doctrines of the divinity of

58. "Preunderstanding," p. 210.
59. "(De)constructing the (Non)being of G⊗d," p. 447.
60. Ibid., p. 448.
61. Ibid., pp. 449–50.

Christ and the resurrection represent a confusion of Hellenistic categories with the Gospel narratives concerning Jesus. Putt, on the other hand, feels that this objection is a matter of Caputo falling back into a modernist, rather than a postmodern, paradigm.[62] While not insisting that Caputo adopt his view that "Jesus of Nazareth was historically and ontically the Son of God enfleshed," Putt asserts that incarnation is not incongruous with Caputo's postmodernism.[63]

Putt says that while the idea of incarnation is not necessarily incompatible with certain Greek myths, it cannot be accepted if one holds the Hellenistic models of GØd as immutable and impassible. He believes that all the problems associated with the traditional attempt to understand how the Son of GØd could be a human being stem from the attempt to maintain the contradictory positions of the deity of Christ and the immutability and impassibility of GØd.[64] In the incarnation, Jesus does not make humanity divine, but makes the divine human. Thus, genuine alterity is present, "not in the facade of change, but in real mutability."[65] Putt acknowledges that his approach does not break completely with ontotheology. He notes the dichotomy in Paul's writing of the incarnation as both *kenosis* and *plerosis*.[66]

The nonbeing of mutability is accompanied by the ultimate expression of nonbeing—the death of the incarnated GØd. Here is the most complete act of divine suffering. Putt holds that Christ's death and resurrection are in some way salvific for humanity. That raises, however, the question of how these miraculous acts produce that salvation. He reports Caputo's rejection of the penal model, whereby Christ suffers the penalty or pays the debt for the sins of sinners. Such an arrangement does not really involve forgiveness. Nothing has been forgiven; the debts have been fully paid. Rather, forgiveness is genuine forgiveness. It is GØd's willingness to cancel the liability. Divine forgiveness involves GØd's declaring that nothing has happened, so nothing is owed. Putt agrees with Caputo's rejection of a penal understanding of atonement. He says, "Caputo is correct when he claims that forgiveness cannot be established upon a foun-

62. Ibid., p. 467.
63. Ibid., p. 468.
64. Ibid., pp. 470–71.
65. Ibid., p. 472.
66. Ibid., pp. 473–75.

dation of revenge and repayment. To forgive is to take a loss, not to
have the debt repaid, to be willing to sacrifice whatever has been
taken away, damaged, or wounded by the offending act."[67] In the
crucifixion, the Father and the Spirit not only suffer with the Son
through the compassion that they feel for one another, but also suffer with him in realizing that the wounds inflicted on him are dealt
by those he came to save. "What the cross reveals, then, about the
divine love is that GØd is powerful enough to sacrifice the divine
seO(l,X)f to the forces of evil and hatred that diametrically opposed
GØd's <u>agape. . . .</u> To say, therefore, that Jesus carries the sin of humanity to the cross is to say that on the cross the extent of the divine
grief is revealed. To say that Jesus suffered the divine wrath is to say
that his fleshly wounds are symbols of the wounded love of the Trinity."[68]

Putt never makes clear the full basis of his theopassionist view of
God. There is no detailed biblical or other documentation. It is regarded as part of the broad sweep of Scripture, or the biblical view.
It almost appears that this is a presupposition brought to the discussion of postmodernism, and the ability of a postmodern view to fit
with it is virtually a criterion for evaluation of postmodernism.

Analytical Summary

Having now noted Putt's comments on the views of other deconstructionists and his own constructive position, it may be helpful to
make explicit some of the salient tenets of that view.

1. There is a clear rejection of the usual form of ontotheology,
   which tries to tie all truth up in a complete system and answer all questions. This means that systematic theology, as
   usually understood, is also regarded as untenable.
2. All forms of foundationalism are rejected, whether rationalist or empiricist.
3. Deconstruction, even that of Derridá, is interpreted in a
   rather conservative fashion, as denying not that language

67. Ibid., p. 477. This death would seem to be vicarious, that is, for the sake of
humans, but not substitutionary. See also B. Keith Putt, "Indignation Toward Evil:
Ricoeur and Caputo on a Theodicy of Protest," *Philosophy Today* 41.3/4 (Fall 1997):
469.
68. Ibid., pp. 478, 479.

has a nonlinguistic reference, but rather that we can know it completely or with certainty.

4. The classical understanding of God as timeless, immutable, and impassible is rejected.
5. Deconstruction is endorsed as a means of refuting the onto-theological understanding of God.
6. Putt's understanding of God—as suffering and responding to human actions and predicaments—is seen to be consistent with deconstruction.
7. The exact relationship of the objective and subjective factors in meaning, and of the cognitive and personal elements in revelation, is rather ambiguous.

Evaluation

There are both points of strength and significant problems in Putt's somewhat unusual evangelical theology.

Positive

1. Putt is to be commended for making a genuine effort to speak to and relate to the contemporary mood. He has seen that some of the traditional ways of presenting the Christian message are not only not being accepted, but are not even understood or heard by contemporary persons.
2. Putt seems to have understood very well the nature of deconstruction. He has read enough to be able to speak from within the world of the deconstructionist.
3. Putt has truly entered into the mood, style, and methodology of deconstruction. Ability to do deconstruction, not merely talk about it, is the clearest sign of understanding.
4. Putt has understood that everyone, at least initially, comes to attempted understanding from a particular perspective and with a particular set of presuppositions.
5. Putt has shown creativity in attempting to apply deconstruction to a sphere and type of theology where it has not been employed previously.
6. Putt makes a genuine effort to be biblical. He seeks to meld biblical revelation with the radical hermeneutics of John Caputo.

Negative

These are, from our perspective, both more numerous and more significant.

1. It is not exactly clear why Putt adopts deconstruction. It appears that in part this is because of the current strength and popularity of the movement. As such, however, that appears to be a case of the "chronological snobbery" that Oden and others have spoken against. If so, then, as Oden, Wells, and others have observed, although claiming to be postmodern, one is actually exhibiting commitment to a major tenet of the modern era, progress, since what is later is better than what is earlier. The ambiguity in Putt's approach is seen in his claim that Jesus used deconstruction. Does this mean that Jesus was a postmodern person? At times, it appears that theopassionism is the non-negotiable, and that deconstruction is utilized because it negates the ontology on which classical orthodoxy has based its view of God. The introduction of the thought of Moltmann, certainly no deconstructionist, into a supposedly deconstructive methodology, seems to support this interpretation. While some recent developments in science and mathematics may indeed argue against the possibility of complete systems, those arguments are found within considerably more systematic frameworks than that of deconstruction.

2. Much of the force of Putt's argument comes from contrasting the Hellenistic model, which is believed to lie behind the traditional view of God with the biblical view, understood as the Hebraic (or Jew/Christian) mentality. This seems to perpetuate one of the elements of the Biblical Theology movement, which flourished about forty years ago. To be sure, there are differences between classical Greek philosophy and biblical religion, but as James Barr demonstrated so forcefully,[69] this is overstated by the theologians of that movement, and with them, by Putt. Barr's conclusions have been widely accepted,[70] and some rebuttal should be given

69. James Barr, *Semantics of Biblical Language* (New York: Oxford University Press, 1961).
70. E.g., Brevard S. Childs, *Biblical Theology in Crisis* (Philadelphia: Westminster, 1970), pp. 70–72.

if one is to continue to hold the old idea of the "distinctive biblical mentality" almost four decades after Barr wrote. If not, one is in danger of propounding an argument that is seriously outdated.

3. The depiction of the classical view of God is either a caricature or a carefully selected variety of that view. Many contemporary evangelical theologians do not hold to immutability and impassibility in the form of the Thomistic view. Some, indeed, explicitly distinguish classical orthodoxy's view of God from that of Thomism.[71] Similarly, extreme types of foundationalism are used to discredit the whole endeavor of offering objective grounds for one's views. This is ironic, since Putt accuses D. A. Carson of caricaturing theopassionism.

4. There is no clear or persuasive justification for Putt's deviation from the full application of the method of deconstruction. Just as Derridá appears to have compromised his method by asserting that there is one thing that cannot be deconstructed, namely, justice, so it is not entirely certain that one can adopt deconstruction but retain some ontotheology (such as the incarnation) without a more vigorous justification. Interestingly, Caputo holds that belief in the incarnation represents the retention of Hellenism, while Putt thinks that this position of Caputo is a carryover of modern ways of thinking. The predicament of deconstruction is that there does not seem to be any obvious way of adjudicating this difference. Without such, these charges sound almost like ad hominems. It could, of course, be asserted that the call for reasoned choices and logical consistency represented in this criticism, as well as in number 1 above, is a modern approach. When, however, one has said that, then it becomes increasingly unclear how one goes about choosing among different types of deconstructive philosophy or theology.

5. The preceding difference suggests that Putt recognizes the importance of presuppositions in disputes of this type. What

71. E.g., Ronald H. Nash, *The Concept of God: An Exploration of Contemporary Difficulties with the Attributes of God* (Grand Rapids: Zondervan, 1983), pp. 19–36.

is not equally operative, here, however, is the acknowledgment of the role of his own presuppositions. The valuing of divine suffering and the aversion to inclusive views (or metanarratives) are significant presuppositions that ought to be acknowledged and justified. Strong Kierkegaardian motifs, for example, seem to lie behind Putt's hostility to ontotheology and metanarratives. If the interpretation of Scripture through Hellenistic presuppositions leads to reading that into the Bible, why does he not acknowledge that his own existentialism, for example, has also been read into the text?

6. Closely akin to this criticism is the fact that this deconstructive theology, like most versions of deconstruction, is seriously in need of deconstruction. Putt proceeds as if this is a neutral and benevolent view, not at all characterized by the attempt to dominate others. On what grounds does it deserve this exemption?

7. Putt consistently asserts that he is trying to preserve the biblical view of God. Unfortunately, however, he gives very little treatment of specific portions of Scripture. What he seems to do is draw broad motifs from Scripture. These are rather heavily disputed, however.

8. It does not appear that Putt has dealt with some of the problems of a theopassionist view such as his. For example, a God who suffers sympathetically and does not necessarily remove all evil, even in the eschaton,[72] seems doomed to perpetual suffering, as Richard Creel has pointed out.[73] Indeed, the better recent philosophical literature, such as that of Creel, is not introduced and interacted with.

9. Finally, some evangelicals will question the sense and extent to which this theology can be labeled evangelical, even of the postmodern, postconservative variety. Certainly, Putt's tenacious insistence on the incarnation, crucifixion, and resurrection preserves essential evangelical doctrinal tenets. It is clear that insofar as one could speak of salvation here, it must be understood as fully of grace. The primacy of Scripture as authority is somewhat more questionable. Putt seems

---

72. "(De)constructing G⊗d," p. 464.
73. Richard E. Creel, *Divine Impassibility: An Essay in Philosophical Theology* (Cambridge: Cambridge University Press, 1986), pp. 123–25.

at times to base his view on some sort of basic intuitions, or on the appeal of certain literary pieces that he examines. The view of atonement is certainly not that of penal substitution, which has often lain at the heart of evangelical theology. And, although salvation as regeneration through faith is central to any meaningful use of the term "evangelical," there seems to be no mention of new birth in his writings.

Part 4

Conclusion

8
Postmodern Apologetics

Can Deconstructed Horses Even Be Led to Water?

We have seen six different responses by claimed evangelicals to the phenomenon of postmodernism. They range from those that are negative about postmodernism to those that are quite favorable and inclined to adopt it. It may be helpful to classify these in terms of different responses to a question posed to a panel of which I was a part at a professional society. The question was: Can deconstructed horses even be led to water? Although we should not equate all postmodernisms with deconstruction, and our concern is not exclusively with apologetics, this is a convenient place to begin the consideration.

The question before us actually involves several elements: the horse; the means of leading (the halter and rope); and the water. Several different answers might be given to this question. I want to outline these, and then give a brief indication of my personal reaction to the question and the options. There are, it appears to me, roughly four answers that can be given, and are being given, to this question.

1. Yes, but it must be deconstructed water. This basically says that the only kind of water that a deconstructed horse will drink, or to which he will let himself be led, is deconstructed water. If the horse is genuinely deconstructed, then the water presented to him must be suited to the horse. This of course involves conceding the truth of deconstruction of the horse. It grants that the horse is deconstructed and that deconstruction is here to stay and must be accepted. In terms of a set of categories that I have borrowed from my doctoral

mentor, William Hordern, and used several times over the years, these persons are not merely translators, but transformers. They are prepared to alter the expression and even the content of the Christian faith if necessary in order to make it acceptable to the postmodern deconstructionist.

A number of the contentions of the deconstructionists conflict with evangelicalism as generally understood. The latter must therefore be adjusted. Among these are the following: the objectivity of truth; a referential understanding of language; a correspondence theory of truth; the existence of "metanarratives"; the presence of some universal qualities of human nature. One theologian who represents and advocates this approach is a person who would not claim to be an evangelical, Mark C. Taylor. Of the persons whose views we have examined in these pages, Keith Putt most strongly represents this approach. Middleton and Walsh also do so, by the way in which they recast the method of utilizing Scripture. And although Stanley Grenz proposes primarily a different methodology, his revisioning of evangelicalism involves some substantive changes as well.

2. Yes, but we must use deconstructed rope. This view may or may not feel that the water needs deconstruction in order to be appealing to deconstructed horses (i.e., that the message needs to be altered). It does maintain, however, that it is necessary to alter the form of leading, that is, the method and means. It is more the form or the style of presentation, rather than the content, that needs to be changed. This would mean, for example, that instead of a propositional presentation, what would be done is to make a narrative approach. Generally speaking, this approach would hold to the objectivity of truth and the relativity of knowledge, but would acknowledge that all knowers are to some extent historically and socially conditioned.

Of the theologians we have examined, Middleton and Walsh, with their advocacy of a narrative presentation of the truth, certainly represent this approach. The same is true of Grenz, with his narrative-shaped and community-based theology.

3. Yes, but the horse is not really deconstructed. This denies that the horse, although it may think it is deconstructed, really is. Consequently, no adjustment, of either the water or the technique of leading, is needed. The same methods of leading horses can be used with deconstructed or postmodern horses, which have been used before.

The world has not really changed all that radically, according to this third response. There is a belief that the deconstructionist is engaged in sort of unintentional self-deception. There are two varieties of this type of response, which we may term, respectively, the kerygmatic and the apologetic.

The kerygmatic variety believes in the self-authenticating character of the biblical message. Usually this is combined with a strong belief in the convicting, illuminating power of the Holy Spirit. Thus, all that needs to be done is to present the truth, and it will bear fruit. To take seriously the idea that humans can cut themselves off so fully from the grace of God that they cannot be reached with a plain presentation of the truth is to concede the point that the deconstructive postmodernist is making, thus, in effect denying the message being presented.

The apologetic variety of this response suggests that we can engage in some of the traditional types of arguments. These may have to be carefully selected, but are still useful. Persons are still rational, despite changes that may have taken place in the world. Consequently, rational arguments can still be utilized.

Of our six case studies, David Wells seems to fit best within this approach. His approach is not apologetic in the traditional sense of the word, but is certainly polemic in its treatment of modernity, especially evangelicalism's concessions to it. He primarily works from a historical basis, seeking to show what evangelicalism has historically been and what it is in danger of becoming.

In a different way, Thomas Oden also falls into this classification. His contention, however, is not that the horse is not postmodern, but that what is often termed postmodernity is actually hypermodernity. It is the extension and expansion of trends that were present within modernity. It is the logical (and tragic) consequence of modernity, taken to an extreme.

4. Yes, but we must first de-deconstruct the horse. This approach says that the horse is deconstructed, but that it is not possible to live on such a basis. There is both a more pessimistic and a more optimistic version of this view. The more pessimistic holds that deconstructed horses simply have to be written off, but that our aim is to be to prevent other, nondeconstructed horses, from being deconstructed. Apologetics, on this view is primarily a defensive endeavor. The more optimistic approach says deconstructed horses can be reached, but they must first be de-deconstructed, and this requires

that they be more thoroughly deconstructed. This is done by pushing such horses to be consistently and thoroughly deconstructed, so that they discover that it is not possible to live on this basis. The problem with deconstructed horses is not that they don't believe enough, but that they believe too much, more than they really ought to be entitled to believe, on their premises.

Clearly, Francis Schaeffer's approach is to be found here. His approach was to push the person to see the outcome of his own position, by removing some of the roof that he had erected to protect himself. It is at this point that the person realizes the impossibility of living in a divided fashion, inconsistent with his basic philosophy, on the one hand, but also inconsistent with his own inherent humanity, on the other. Not until this point is reached can the traditional type of positive argument for the Christian faith be made.

The matter of a thorough response to postmodernism requires a much more extensive treatment than we can give here, and will be the subject of a much larger work to follow. At this point, however, I believe I see the beginnings of the contour of such a response.

For myself, I believe that a combination of forms of response number 2 and response number 4 holds the most promise. We are talking here, not about going all the way with number 2, but taking some aspects of it on a provisional basis. One insight that postmodernism has correctly seen is that all of our knowledge is held from a particular perspective, or to put it differently, is based on our own presuppositions. Their critique here is well taken. I am frequently impressed, in reading books and reviews, with how frequently the author fails to recognize his or her own presuppositions. This is especially a problem for those who work within a strong ideological tradition, where the critique of the other position assumes the correctness of one's own. It is, in effect, a tacit way of saying, "You are wrong, because your view differs from mine."

What we do at this point is, of course, crucial. If we simply accept this conditioned nature of our perspective, then we have relatively little grounds for contending that one view is more correct than another. This would seem to be the direction in which at least in theory, the typical postmodernist should have to go. The alternative is to recognize the perspective nature of one's own view, but attempt to eliminate as much as possible its subjectivity, moving toward the idea of objectivity.

This means that we will need to cross the bridge to where the horse is, rather than standing on our side of the bridge and trying to coax the horse to come to us. Eventually, of course, we must bring the horse across the bridge, but that may not be possible initially. We will need to enter into the other person's perspective, to think from his or her presuppositions. It means that we will have to listen to the deconstructionist, rather than just talking, which tends to be an occupational disease of both clergypersons and sometimes of lay Christians. There is a point in the deconstructionist's contention of relativity, and that is that we all see reality from our own perspective or our own presuppositions. The truth is objective, but our understanding may be in part affected by the angle from which we look at it. We will need to look through our deconstructionist's eyes long enough to understand why for him or her the view makes good sense. Then we will better understand how to relate the message to the person in a way that can be understood. I once heard Myron Augsburger say that unless we so immerse ourselves in the Muslim way of viewing things that we are tempted to become Muslims, we will never reach the Muslim.

One of the most valuable courses I took in college, although I did not see it that way at the time, was a course in debate. The value of it was that one week I and my partner would argue one side of the issue and the next week we would have to take the opposite side. Something of that approach is what I think may help us here. Because we have the truth, the absolute truth as revealed by God, we may be tempted to feel that we should simply tell people that, and there is no point in listening to their errors. But the way to respond to the authoritarianism of some deconstructionists is not to be similarly dogmatic.

Deconstructionism is correct in contending that ideologies, especially inclusive ones, can and sometimes are used against people and groups as means of getting one's way. One of the responses to this is to take the time to listen, to honestly consider the dialogue partner's contentions, and to admit when we are wrong or in need of modification.

In initiating conversation with a deconstructionist, we may need to modify the way in which we do the leading or present the message. This may mean that a more narrative presentation, not in the hermeneutical or heuristic but in the communicational sense of narrative, will have to be the beginning of the conversation.

The other approach that I believe can be used partially is the fourth. Like Schaeffer, I believe that we must push deconstructionists to the end of their view, to live out consistently that position, believing that no one could actually live on the basis of such a view. I believe that we may need to help the deconstructionist "hit bottom," like an alcoholic, before there will be any significant sense of need to move beyond that approach.

When we do that, we will find some frustration and resistance, but it will also bring to the surface the impossibility of living consistently with a thoroughly radical postmodern view. This was brought out rather dramatically in the case of Derridá. John Searle wrote a response to an article of Derridá's, challenging and criticizing several of his conceptions.[1] Searle's article was eleven pages in length. In his *ninety-three*-page reply, Derridá objected that Searle's statement had been unfair to him, and had at several points misunderstood and misstated his position. He even asserted at one point that what he had meant should have been clear and obvious to Searle.[2] I consider that an incredibly nondeconstructionist, nonpostmodern response for someone who maintains that the meaning of a text is not in the author's intention, but in what the reader finds it saying to him or her. Michael Fisher observes that some of Derridá's followers are embarrassed by this inconsistency between Derridá's profession and his actual practice in this article.[3] Yet John Ellis maintains that those same disciples "generally have also done exactly what embarassed them when they saw Derrida doing it (i.e., they too routinely accuse Searle of misunderstanding, missing the point of, and misstating Derridá's position)."[4] Similarly, Frank Lentricchia accuses the "Yale group" of misconstruing Derridá's writing by "ignoring . . . an important part of the author's intention."[5] If, however, the position of deconstruction is that the author's intention does not control the meaning of his or her text, then this would seem to be an inconsistent

1. John Searle, "Reiterating the Differences: Reply to Derrida," *Glyph* 1 (1977): 198–208.

2. Jacques Derridá, "Limited, Inc., abc," *Glyph* 2 (1977): 162–254.

3. Michael Fisher, *Does Deconstruction Make Any Difference?* (Bloomington: Indiana University Press, 1985), pp. 40–41.

4. John M. Ellis, *Against Deconstruction* (Princeton, N.J.: Princeton University Press, 1989), p. 14, n. 10.

5. Frank Lentricchia, *After the New Criticism* (Chicago: University of Chicago Press, 1980), p. 170.

position. We must help finish deconstructing the horse, before the horse can be de-deconstructed, or reconstructed.

One of the objections that will of course be raised to this technique is that by calling attention to logical inconsistency, it assumes the very type of objective, rational logic that it supposedly is trying to establish. We must however, ask a question that it seems to me is not really being asked by the participants in this discussion. What kind of language are we using when we talk about language? When a deconstructionist discusses deconstruction, is he or she really using deconstructed language? If such were the case, the deconstructionist would probably remain silent, or at least would not expect anyone else to understand and agree with him or her. I would contend that at bottom, all views, even those of postmodernists, insofar as they attempt to communicate their tenets and to persuade others of them, are assuming some basic rationality that is not distinctive of the modern approach.

One other way of doing this is to show what consequences flow from deconstructing meaning and language. What happens is often a new kind of authoritarianism, such as is found in Political Correctness, where only one answer is permitted. Thus, deconstruction may lead to a new form of oppression. There is a strong element of truth in the deconstructionists' contention that ideologies can be used oppressively. Deconstruction itself is not exempt from this theory, however. Such horses must be de-deconstructed.

Index

Millard J. Erickson is Distinguished Professor of Theology at Baylor University's Truett Seminary and at Western Seminary, Portland. He is a leading evangelical spokesman with numerous volumes to his credit, including *Christian Theology, God in Three Persons, The Word Became Flesh, The Evangelical Left,* and *Where Is Theology Going?*